UNDERSTANDING BASIC ENGLISH GRAMMAR
FOR UNIVERSITY STUDENTS

대학생을 위한
기초영문법의 이해

김우형 · 김태영 지음

TO IMPROVE
VERB
TO ACHIEVE
PRACTICE
GERUNDS
SUGGEST
TO PRESENT

GS인터비전

머 리 말

현재 국제화 흐름 속에 글로벌 인재로서 성장하기 위해서는 글로벌 사회에서 요구하는 글로벌 소양과 더불어 영어로 능숙하게 소통할 수 있는 능력이 절대적으로 요구되고 있습니다. 국제 사회가 요구하는 의사소통 능력을 키우기 위해서는 먼저 영어 문장의 구조와 문법, 필수 어휘들을 숙지하고 익히는 것이 중요하다고 생각합니다. 특히 영어 초보 수험생은 기본적인 문법과 구조, 중요 어휘들을 잘 이해한 후, 차근차근 정선된 연습 문제를 통해 익혀 나간다면 총체적인 영어 능력을 향상시키는 데 큰 도움이 될 수 있을 것입니다.

본 교재 "대학생을 위한 기초 영문법의 이해"는 이러한 영어 초보 수험생들을 위해 만들어졌습니다. 많은 고등학생과 대학생이 수많은 TOEIC 교재나 TOEFL, TEPS 교재 중 어떤 교재를 선택할지 몰라 주저하는 모습을 종종 보았습니다. 본 교재는 단어, 기초 영문법, 독해 문제 연습을 통해 영어 초보 수험자인 고등학생과 대학생들의 영어 실력을 향상시키고, 각종 영어 공인 시험과 공무원 시험을 대비할 수 있도록 만든 기본서입니다. 또한 영어에 대한 기본적인 지식을 가진 대학생들이 대학원 진학 시험, 경찰 공무원 영어시험, 대학 편입학 시험, TOEIC, IBT TOEFL, TEPS 등의 시험을 완벽하게 준비할 수 있도록 Sentence Structure, Grammar Practice와 Vocabulary 파트로 문제를 구성하여 교재를 만들었습니다.

본 교재가 많은 영어 초보 수험생들에게 다양한 영어 실전 문제를 풀어 볼 수 있는 기회를 제공함으로써, 난이도 있는 영어 문제를 처음 접해 보는 영어 초보자들이 영어를 활용하고 숙지할 수 있는 자신감을 극대화시키는 데 큰 도움을 줄 수 있을 것이라 확신합니다.

저자 김우형, 김태영 씀

차 례

Chapter 1. VERB

Chapter 2. TENSE

Chapter 3. NOUN

Chapter 4. PRONOUN

Chapter 5. ADJECTIVE

Chapter 6. ADVERB

Chapter 7. VOICE

Chapter 8. INFINITIVE

Chapter 9. GERUND

Chapter 10. PARTICIPLE

Chapter 11. PREPOSITION

Chapter 12. CONJUNCTION

Chapter 13. RELATIVE PRONOUN

CHAPTER 1

VERB

I. Grammar Focus

A. 1형식 동사(S+V)

~에 가다: **go**, run, fly, rise, leave for, head for

~에 오다: **come**, decline, happen, occur, rain, snow

~에 머물러 있다: **exist**, live, stand, stay

1. 완전자동사(동사+전치사)

His father's illness **added to** his troubles. (=increased)

At last he **arrived in** Seoul. (=reached)

She failed to **reply to** my question. (=answer)

Death **waits for** all men. (=await)

He **started from** New York a few days ago. (=left)

You must **apologize to** your sister for being so rude.

She **complains of** my being late for working.

2. 완전자동사(의미상)

Anything **will do.** (=be good enough)

Honesty **pays.** (=be beneficial to)

The tool will **work well.** (=beneficial to)

This problem **matters.** (=be of consequence)

B. 2형식동사(S+V+C)

-**be**, **become**, **remain** (= stay)

-seem/appear, prove/turn out, remain to be seen, remain competitive

-look, smell, taste, sound + 형용사

1. 불완전자동사(동사+형용사)

(feel, sound, smell, taste, look, seem, appear, continue, remain, keep, prove...)

Mary **looks beautiful** in her pink dress.

The rose **smells sweet.**

A good medicine **tastes bitter** to the mouth.

She **kept silent** to the last.

2. get, come, grow + to부정사(~하게 되다)

She **came to fall** in love with him.

How did you **get to know** the fact?

Tom **became to be** aware of the flat tire.(x)

C. 3형식 동사(S+V+O)

1. 완전타동사

A boy of eighteen is **approaching** manhood.

I **await** your instructions.

The United States **comprises** 50 states.

Edelweiss, Edelweiss, every morning you **greet** me.

John is going to **marry** Jane.

Don't **mention** it.

She **resembles** her mother.

We **discuss**ed the matter. 〈-〉 I **discuss**ed with them.

She **attended** the meeting 〈-〉 He **attended to** your lesson.

〈-〉 She has many servants **attending on** her.

The bullets **enter**ed the wall. 〈-〉 He **entered into** conversation with her.

2. 완전타동사(도난, 박탈동사)

He robbed(deprived) her **of** her money.

(=She was robbed of her money by him.)

The burglar **stole** his books **from** him.

(= His books were stolen from him by the burglar.)

The post office ⎤
The bank ⎦ was robbed last night.

3. 설명 동사(사물 + to 사람)

(explain, announce, demonstrate, describe, suggest, propose, say, confess, introduce...)

He **explained** the problem **to me** at once.

Mary **introduced** her sister **to** Tom.

He **suggested to her** that they go to the movies.

She **said to me** that I was very busy.

4. 용법에 주의를 요하는 동사

1) I hope an early start. (x)

I hope for an early start. (o)

I hope seeing you again. (x)

I hope to see you again. (o)

I hope you to come soon. (x)

I hope that you will come soon. (o)

2) I want that you will do it at once. (x)

I want you to do it at once. (o)

3) I warned that she should not go. (x)

I warned her not to go. (o)

I warned him that it was dangerous. (o)

4) She says to try her best. (x)

She says that she will try her best. (o)

He said the statement to be true. (x)

He said that the statement was true. (o)

D. 4형식 동사(S+V+IO+DO)

- **give**, **offer**, **send**, **bring**, ask, buy, cost, lend, show, tell
- **inform**, **notify**, **assure**, **remind**

1. 4형식에서 3형식으로 전환

If you are going to the public library, please **bring** two or three good novels to me.

We **played** a trick on him.

Play a tune for me.

I'll **play** a game of chess with you.

2. envy, forgive, save, cost 등의 동사

I **envy you your power** of saying things so immediately.

I'll **forgive you your sin.**

Careless driving may **cost you your life.**

E. 5형식 동사(S+V+O+OC)

1) 형/~ing/p.p를 목적어보어로 = **make, keep, find**

2) to부정사를 목적어보어로: (동사들이 모두 미래의 뜻)

설득류 : persuade, convince, encourage, motivate, compel, force, tell, teach

허락류 : permit, allow, enable

바램류 : expect, want, would like, require

권함류 : cause, remind, invite, advise, ask

3) 원형동사를 목적어 보어로:

- **사역동사** + 목적어 + 원형, p.p (let, make, have)
- **get** + 목적어 + to원형, p.p (준사역동사)
- 지각동사 + 목적어 + 원형, -ing, p.p (see, hear, feel)

1. 장려동사(~을 하도록 하다) + O + to 부정사

(encourage, persuade, enable, permit, allow, urge, tell, advise, order, …)

Mary's friends **encouraged** her **to solve** the problem.

His father **permits** him **to go** out for a walk.

The doctor **advised** her **to keep** good health.

My mother **persuaded** me **to overcome** the difficulty.

2. 금지동사(~을 못하도록 하다) + O + from -ing

(discourage, dissuade, prevent, hinder, prohibit, keep, disable, …)

My teacher **dissuaded** us **from going** out.

What **prevented** you **from coming** here?

He **disabled** her **from the execution** of his plans.

The king **forbade** the song **to be sung.** (주의)

3. make + oneself + -ed

He **made himself understood** in English.

The speaker couldn't **make himself heard.**

Mary must **make herself known** about the problem.

4. think + of류 동사 + O + as

(think of, look upon, regard, consider, view, acknowledge, …)

We **regard** the dove **as** the symbol of peace.

They **think of** him **as** wise.

He **looked on** him **as** wise.

I **acknowledged** myself **as** defeated.

F. 주의할 동사의 용법

1. 혼동하기 쉬운 동사의 활용

lie - lied - lied (거짓말 하다)

lie - lay - lain (눕다, 위치하다)

lay - laid - laid (놓다, 눕히다, 알을 낳다)

fall - fell - fallen (떨어지다)

fell - felled - felled (쓰러뜨리다)

find - found - found (발견하다)

found - founded - founded (설립하다)

saw - sawed - sawn (톱질하다)

sow - sowed - sown (씨뿌리다)

sew - sewed - sewn (꿰매다)

wind - wound - wound (감다, 구불거리다)

wound - wounded - wounded (상처를 입히다)

rise - rose - risen (일어나다)

raise - raised - raised (일으키다, 손을 들다, 제기하다, 키우다)

2. 혼동하기 쉬운 동사의 활용

Can I **borrow** your book for two weeks? (빌려오다)

Would you please **lend** me 10 dollars? (빌려주다)

He **caught** influenza. (병에 걸리다)

He **had** influenza. (병으로 고생하다)

She got up and **put** on her blue dress. (동작표시)

Did you **wear** your new dress that night? (상태표시)

I **doubt** that our team will win. (~아닐 것이라고 생각하다)

I **suspect** that he is a liar. (~일거라고 생각하다)

John **won** the chess game easily. (게임에서 이기다)

He easily **beat** George at chess. ("사람"을 이기다)

II. Sentence Structure

1. The car _____ to my uncle.
   (A) belongs (B) belong
   (C) are belonging (D) belonging

2. The bus _____ every twenty minutes.
   (A) run (B) runs
   (C) are running (D) running

3. I _____ to watch comedies on TV.
   (A) liking (B) likes
   (C) am liking (D) like

4. They _____ at two o'clock tomorrow.
   (A) arrived (B) have arrived
   (C) are arriving (D) arriving

5. He _____ a lot of money with him.
   (A) is having (B) has
   (C) have (D) had had

6. She _____ sick.
   (A) is (B) sees
   (C) has (D) does

7. What do you _____ ?
   (A) will (B) is
   (C) do (D) be

연구 및 정답

1. (A) 본문의 동사가 필요하며 3인칭 단수.
2. (B) 본문의 주어인 The bus 다음에 동사가 필요하며, 3인칭 단수.
3. (D) 본문의 동사가 필요하며 주어 I에 맞는 동사는?
4. (C) 본문에 미래 동사가 필요하다.
5. (B) 문장의 술부가 요구됨.
6. (A) 문장의 형용사를 보어로 갖는 동사가 필요하다.
7. (C) 의문문의 경우 do는 일반동사를 받는다.

1. Milk proteins _____ for their high nutritional content.
   (A) valued (B) are valued
   (C) are they valued (D) to be valued

2. According to one definition, "avoidance" _____ behavior induced by adverse stimuli.
   (A) when (B) in
   (C) that (D) is

3. Cedars _____ a particular variety of aromatic wood that repels insects.
   (A) having yields (B) yielding
   (C) yields (D) yield

4. He _____ a pioneer in American textile design and interior decoration.
   (A) who (B) as
   (C) was (D) often

5. Hawthorne and Poe _____ in the development of American short story.
   (A) who were leaders (B) they were leaders
   (C) were both leaders (D) who as leaders

6. Refrigerating meats _____ the spread of bacteria.
   (A) retards (B) retarding
   (C) to retard (D) is retarded

7. At room temperature, calcium chloride _____ a white solid.
   (A) as (B) is
   (C) that is (D) although

연구 및 정답

1. (B) 주어 Milk proteins에 사람들이 가치를 부여하므로 B가 적합하다.
2. (D) 본문의 주어인 avoidance 다음에 동사가 필요하다.
3. (D) 본문의 동사가 필요하며 주어가 복수명사이다.
4. (C) 본문에 동사가 필요하다.
5. (C) 문장의 술부가 요구됨.
6. (A) 문장의 동사가 필요하다.
7. (B) 문장의 동사가 필요하다.

1. Igneous rock _____ from the cooling and solidification of molten matter from the Earth's interior.
   (A) being originated (B) have originated
   (C) originates (D) originating

2. Work _____ to generate electricity.
   (A) to be done (B) it is done
   (C) done by it (D) must be done

3. The great Chicago fire in October, 1871, _____ much of the city and left about 100,000 people homeless.
   (A) that it destroyed (B) that destroyed
   (C) was destroyed (D) destroyed

4. "John got an A in Chemistry." "I _____ that he is very bright."
   (A) had heard (B) will have heard
   (C) hear (D) am hearing

5. "What's your opinion?" "It is imperative that they _____ there on time."
   (A) should (B) shall
   (C) be (D) can be

6. Muscles _____ bones by pulling on tendons.
   (A) of moving (B) move
   (C) moving (D) to move

7. Social reformer Jane Adams _____ a prominent role in the formation of the National Progressive party in 1912.
   (A) playing (B) who played
   (C) played (D) to play

연구 및 정답

1. (C) 문의 동사가 빠져있으며 주어가 3인칭 단수임.
2. (D) 문의 동사가 빠져있으며 주어인 work은 행위의 주체가 될 수 없으므로 수동태가 요구된다.
3. (D) 문의 주어는 있으나 동사가 빠져있다. 빈칸 다음에 명사 상당어구가 오므로 타동사 형태이어야 한다. C는 수동태이므로 타동사 성질이 없어짐.
4. (C) 종속절의 시제가 현재임에 유의할 것. 경험의 완료대신에 기본시제를 표시한 문장이다. 동사 hear는 진행형 시제를 취할 수 없다.
5. (C) It is+필연(당연, 의무)+that S+(should)동사원형.
6. (B) 동사 필요.
7. (C) 문의 동사가 빠져있으며, 1912년이므로 과거시제.

Ⅲ. Grammar Practice

1. Exercise to be important for good health.
A B C D

2. Sports fans cheering when they watch their favorite athletes on TV.
A B C D

3. A pineapple to have a hard, brown covering.
A B C D

4. Most children to like to play with sand.
A B C D

5. A tree growing more in wet years than in dry years.
A B C D

6. When bears walk, they looking clumsy and slow.
A B C D

7. People around the world using computers every day.
A B C D

연구 및 정답

1. (A) Excercise라는 주어에 동사가 필요하다.
2. (A) Sports fans가 주어, 다음에 올 것은 술부이다.
3. (B) 이 문장에서 동사는?
4. (B) children의 동사가 요구된다.
5. (B) tree다음에 오는 것은 동사.
6. (C) 주어 they 그 다음에는 동사, 동사의 적절한 형태는?
7. (B) 이 문장에서 동사는?

1. Bill Gates creating(A) Microsoft because(B) he wanted to sell his(C) program for(D) PCs.

2. When it has(A) six weeks old(B), a young(C) squirrel leaves the nest and starts(D) to look for food.

3. Grass(A) seeds be(B) tiny specks and thus can be(C) carried far distances by the wind(D).

4. Generally(A), the summers in Pennsylvania have(B) very hot and(C) the winters are extremely(D) cold.

5. In the twentieth(A) century, elementary(B) algebra has given away(C) to modern, or abstract(D) algebra.

6. The way of reasoning(A) whereby people do(B) conclusions by logical(C) inference from given(D) premises is called the deductive method.

7. Wampum serviced(A) as money for(B) Native Americans and colonists(C) during the early(D) settlement of North America.

연구 및 정답

1. (A) 본문에 동사가 필요.
2. (A) have동사와 be동사의 성질에 관한 문제. has → is.
3. (B) be → are.
4. (B) have동사와 be동사의 성질에 관한 문제. very hot로 보아 B를 are로 고쳐야 한다.
5. (C) 동사구 문제. give way to.
6. (B) 동사구 문제. make a conclusion: 결론을 내리다. do → make.
7. (A) 동사구 문제. serve as: ~로 사용되다. 근무하다. serviced → served.

Ⅳ. Vocabulary

※ Choose the one which has the closest meaning with the underlined part.

1. There has been no twentieth-century anthropologist more <u>celebrated</u> or more controversial than Margaret Mead.
   (A) imaginative (B) hard-working
   (C) distinguished (D) strong-minded
2. The <u>concept</u> of camping as we know it today comes from certain Native American tribes.
   (A) equipment (B) position
   (C) revival (D) notion
3. Water is <u>constantly</u> at work altering the appearance of the Earth.
   (A) covertly (B) creatively
   (C) unceasingly (D) insidiously
4. Some of the limitations encountered by single-celled creatures are avoided if numerous cells <u>cooperate</u> as a multicellular individual.
   (A) comply with (B) compete with
   (C) work together as (D) specialize as
5. The works of novelists Joyce Carol Oats are moving chronicles of <u>contemporary</u> life in the United States.
   (A) simultaneous (B) controversial
   (C) modern (D) temperate
6. When <u>completely</u> fermented, apple cider turns to vinegar.
   (A) slowly (B) totally
   (C) regularly (D) chemically
7. The sense of taste is special in that it is <u>closely</u> related to the sense of smell.
   (A) justifiably (B) intimately
   (C) subtly (D) involuntarily

연구

1. celebrated: famous, distinguished.
2. concept: thought, notion, idea, opinion.
3. constantly: always, without stopping, continual.
4. cooperate: work-together, collaborate.
5. contemporary: modern.
6. complete: whole, entire, thorough.
7. close: near, approaching, imminent.

정답

1. C 2. D 3. C 4. C 5. C 6. B 7. B

1. The representative was asked to verify his earlier statement.
   (A) confirm (B) repeat
   (C) withdraw (D) modify

2. Bread has been a staple of the human diet since prehistoric times.
   (A) great delicacy (B) basic part
   (C) fastener (D) highlight

3. The construction of a bridge calls for a lot of money.
   (A) provides (B) supplies
   (C) requires (D) visits

4. How could such a thing have been brought about?
   (A) considered (B) continued
   (C) produced (D) suspected

5. The man kept his head throughout all the excitement.
   (A) was nodding (B) became excited
   (C) remained calm (D) sat straight

6. America's emphasis on the importance of education for everyone has spurred scientific research.
   (A) spurned (B) encourage
   (C) supplanted (D) endangered

7. A coaster sled is made of wood, has metal runners, and is steered by a crossbar.
   (A) spanned (B) supported
   (C) guided (D) powered

연구

1. verify: confirm, prove, support.
2. staple: important, principle, main.
3. call for: demand. require.
4. bring about: produce, result in.
5. keep one's head: remain calm.
6. spur: urge, goad, prod, provoke.
7. steer: guide, drive, manage, handle.

정답

1. A 2. B 3. C 4. C 5. C 6. B 7. C

CHAPTER 2

TENSE

I. Grammar Focus

A. 시제표

	과거	현재	미래
기본 3시제	-ed, 불규칙동사 과거형	원형동사, 원형(e)s	will/shall+동.원
기본 3진행형	was/were+ing	am/are/is+ing	will/shall+be+ing
완료형	had+p.p	have/has+p.p	will/shall+have+p.p
완료 진행형	had been+ing	have/has+been-ing	will/shall+have been-ing

B. 현재시제(Present Tense)

She **likes** him, but she doesn't love him. (현재의 사실)

The child **cries** whenever she goes to the dentist's. (현재의 습관)

The earth **moves** round the sun. (불변의 진리·격언)

The examination **begins** at 9 : 00 a.m. tomorrow morning. (미래의 예정·계획)

I will stay at home **if it rains tomorrow**. (미래의 대용: 시간·조건부사절에서 쓰인다)

Key Point 1

시간·조건표시 명사절·형용사절에서는 미래·미래완료를 그대로 사용

I don't know when she **will come** again.

I wonder if we **will be able to see** Mary.

The time will come when we **will travel** to the moon.

Key Point 2

현재완료형을 대신하는 현재형(hear, is(are) told, learn, say…

I **hear(=have heard)** that he was successful.

She **says** he doesn't want to see you.

C. 과거시제(Past Tense)

I **went** after him, but I lost him in the crowd. (과거의 동작·상태)

She **would spend** every money she earned on clothing. (과거의 습관)

Did you ever **visit** Disneyland? (과거의 경험)

My teacher said that the French Revolution **broke out** in 1789. (역사적 사실)

Key Point 1

접속사 when, before, after, as soon as에 의해 시간상의 전후가 분명할 때 과거를 과거완료로 대신 사용할 수 있다.

For some time after I **went(=had gone)** to bed, I could not sleep.

That happened before I **met** you.

Key Point 2

부사(구) 중 "ago, just now, when, …"은 과거시제와 사용

The train started 10 minutes ago.
The train had started 10 minutes before.

I have just finished it.
I finished it just now.

When have you met him,(X)
When did you meet him,(O)

D. 미래시제(Future Tense)

I **will be** fifteen years old next year. (미래의 동작이나 상태)

You **shall go** there. (말하는 사람의 의지)

I **will** never **see** such a beautiful sunrise again. (듣는 사람의 의향)

Key Point 1

미래를 표시하는 준조동사

When **are** you **going to** get married?
The taxi is here and we **are about to** leave.
There **is to be** an investigation.
He is **certain to address** the meeting.

Key Point 2

왕래발착동사(arrive, come, go, leave, start)는 현재 또는 현재진행형으로 미래를 표시한다.

The train **leaves(=is leaving)** tonight from Chicago.
The plane **is taking off** at 5:20.
The president **is coming to** the UN this week.

E. 현재완료(Present Perfect Tense)

We have never seen the lion. (경험: ever, never, already, often, once 등의 부사 동반)

I have just finished my homework. (완료: just, now, this morning 등의 부사 동반)

How long have you been in Korea? (계속: for~, since~기간어구동반)

I have bought a new car. (결과)

Please wait until I have eaten lunch. (시간 ·조건 부사절에서는 미래완료 대신 현재완료 사용)

Key Point 1

왕래발착 동사의 현재완료도 "be+p.p"로 대신 사용할 수 있다.

Winter is **come**. = Winter **has come**.
She **is gone**. = She **has gone**.
All hope **is gone** = All hope **has gone**.

Key Point 2

have been to : ~에 갔다 왔다.
have been in : ~에 간적이 있다.
have gone to : ~에 가고 없다.

I **have been to** the station.
How long **have** you **been in** Seoul?
John isn't in. He **has gone to** the movies again.
"Is he here?" - "No, he **has gone to** Paris."

Key Point 3

"주어"가 ~한지 "시간"이 지났다.

She has been dead for ten years(=these ten years).
→ She died ten years ago.
→ Ten years have passed since she died.
→ It is ten years since she died.

F. 과거완료(Past Perfect Tense)

He had to return the book which he **had borrowed** from the library last month.
(대과거 : 과거보다 먼저 일어난 일)

He **had written** five letters by lunch-time. (완료)

He **had never been** abroad before he was forty. (경험)

By the time we got to the airport, our plane **had already left.** (결과)

He **had been** sick for a week when he was to the hospital. (계속)

Key Point 1

「~하자마자」 의 표현방법

He had **no sooner** seen the police **than** he ran away.
No sooner had he seen the police **than** he ran away.
He had **scarcely(hardly)** seen the police **when (before)** he ran away.
Scarcely(Hardly) had he seen the police **when** he ran away.
As soon as he saw the police, he ran away.
(=**The moment** = **The minute**)
Immediately he saw the police, he ran away.
On seeing the police, he ran away.

Key Point 2

과거에 이루지 못한 소망 표현

He hoped to have become a doctor. : s + 소망동사의 과거형 + to have p.p
He was to have become a doctor. : s + be동사의 과거형 + to have p.p
He had hoped to become a doctor. : s + had p.p + to Root~
He had hoped that he would become a doctor. : s + 소망동사의 과거 + that절
He hoped to become a doctor, but he couldn't. : s + 소망동사의 과거형 + to Root~ but + 부정

G. 미래완료 시제(Future Perfect Tense)

미래완료는 명백히 미래 어구가 나타나 있는 문장에 쓴다.

That baby **will have slept** four hours by noon.

You **will have recovered** from the shock by now.

H. 진행시제(Progressive Tense)

John **is going** down. (현재진행)

What **were** you **doing** when I telephoned you? (과거진행)

This time tomorrow we **will be flying** over the Pacific. (미래진행)

He **is playing** a violin solo next. (작정된 가까운 미래)

The postman **is always putting** your letters in my letter box. (반복적인 진행)

Key Point 3

진행시제를 사용하지 못하는 동사

상태동사(resemble, look, be, appear, …)
지각동사(hear, see, smell, …)
소유동사(have, own, belong, …)
인식동사(know, believe, understand, …)
감정동사(love, hate, like, …)

Are you seeing the house over there? (X)
Are you hearing a pin drop?(X)

cf) He **is seeing** the sight of Seoul. (관광하다) (O)
She **was hearing** prof. Park's lecture. (강의를 듣다) (O)
We're **having** breakfast. (먹다) (O)

1. 주장, 명령, 요구, 제안, 충고를 나타내는 동사, 형용사, 명사가 있으면 원형동사가 정답.

(예, insist, recommend, request, suggest, imperative, suggestion, recommendation 등)

이성 판단의 형용사도 마찬가지 =essential, necessary, important

He requested that she should attend the party.

It is necessary that you (should) do it.

He insisted that she (should) change her clothes.

He insisted that she changed her clothes. (사실주장)

II. Sentence Structure

1. Last quarter the rate of inflation _____ by 5 percent.
   (A) has risen
   (B) was risen
   (C) rose
   (D) raised

2. By the time he _____, he will have saved a great amount of money.
   (A) will retire
   (B) has retired
   (C) had retired
   (D) retires

3. Five years ago, he _____ president of the company.
   (A) became
   (B) would become
   (C) has become
   (D) had become

4. As soon as the goods _____, I will give them to you.
   (A) is arriving
   (B) arrive
   (C) arrived
   (D) will arrive

5. We are going to have a short meeting when the sales director _____ back.
   (A) came
   (B) is coming
   (C) have come
   (D) comes

6. We _____ out for lunch at 12:00 every day.
   (A) are going
   (B) go
   (C) are go
   (D) have gone

7. The board of directors decided that it _____ necessary to find a sales manager.
   (A) were
   (B) is
   (C) was
   (D) has been

연구 및 정답

1. (C) last로 보아 과거시제이다.
2. (D) 시간, 조건의 부사절에서는 미래시제는 현재시제로 표현.
3. (A) ago는 과거시제.
4. (B) 시간, 조건의 부사절에서는 미래시제는 현재시제로 표현.
5. (D) 시간, 조건의 부사절에서는 미래시제는 현재시제로 표현.
6. (B) every day는 현재시제.
7. (C) 주절의 시제가 과거이면 종속절은 과거 or 과거완료.

1. Since last year, a lot of companies _____ a difficult time financially.
   (A) experience (B) had experienced
   (C) will have experienced (D) have experienced

2. By the end of next year, the government _____ many positions for exceptional students.
   (A) will have created (B) has created
   (C) created (D) will have been created

3. We'll start when he _____ ready.
   (A) will (B) will is
   (C) will be (D) is

4. We _____ at a party two months ago.
   (A) meet (B) met
   (C) have met (D) meeting

5. So far, there _____ no word from them.
   (A) is (B) was
   (C) has (D) has been

6. When I called on her, Mary _____ her room.
   (A) clean (B) cleans
   (C) cleaning (D) was cleaning

7. On Saturdays, I _____ tennis and my wife goes hiking.
   (A) play (B) played
   (C) have played (D) playing

연구 및 정답

1. (D) since, for 등은 현재완료 구문에 어울린다.
2. (A) 내년 말 때까지는 미래완료이다.
3. (D) 시간, 조건의 부사절에서는 미래시제는 현재시제로 표현.
4. (B) ago는 과거시제.
5. (D) so far는 현재완료.
6. (D) 과거의 어느 특정 시점 즉, 순간적, 일시적인 시점은 과거 진행임.
7. (A) 토요일마다, 늘, 항상은 현재시제.

1. Vitamin C, discovered in 1932, _____ first vitamin for which the molecular structure was established.
   (A) the
   (B) was the
   (C) as the
   (D) being the

2. "When will they leave?" "They _____ very soon."
   (A) do leave
   (B) are leaving
   (C) have left
   (D) leave

3. I _____ three hours when my sister appeared.
   (A) was waiting
   (B) have waited
   (C) had been waiting
   (D) have been waiting

4. Mr. Nixon _____ here in Seoul since the fifth of January.
   (A) was
   (B) had been
   (C) will be
   (D) has been

5. It will not be long before fall _____.
   (A) comes
   (B) will have come
   (C) came
   (D) will come

6. He said that he _____ the book.
   (A) has already read
   (B) reads
   (C) had already read
   (D) already read

7. "Is she here?"
   "No, she _____ Tokyo on business."
   (A) has been to
   (B) had gone to
   (C) has gone to
   (D) has been in

연구 및 정답

1. (B) 1932년 과거시제임.
2. (B) 가까운 미래시제는 현재진행으로 표현.
3. (C) 과거이전 시각의 계속적인 표현.
4. (D) since 앞의 시제는 현재완료가 적합하다.
5. (A) 시간 부사절, 미래시제 대신 현재시제로.
6. (C) 과거 이전 시제.
7. (C) 현재의 결과를 표현.

Ⅲ. Grammar Practice

1. In 1989, there(A) is(B) a big(C) earthquake in(D) San Francisco.

2. People are recycle(A) aluminum(B) cans and(C) glass bottles(D).

3. Steven Spielberg has win(A) the(B) directors award(C) in(D) Hollywood once.

4. In(A) 1879 Alexander Graham Bell has decided(B) to emigrate(C) to America(D).

5. More(A) and(B) more people are use(C) credit cards(D).

6. Since the(A) 1980s VCRs changed(B) our(C) culture very much(D).

7. A(A) druggist, John Pemberton, invent(B) Coca-Cola(C) in(D) 1886.

연구 및 정답

1. (B) 1989년 볼 때 과거시제 필요.
2. (A) 현재 진행형 be+ing.
3. (A) 현재 완료형 have(has)+pp.
4. (B) 1879년으로 볼 때 과거시제임.
5. (C) 현재 진행형 be+ing.
6. (B) since, for는 현재완료형을 받는다. 과거에서부터 현재까지의 경험, 계속을 표현.
7. (B) 1886년은 과거시제로 표현.

1. A desert area that has been(A) without water(B) for six years will still(C) bloom when rain will come(D).

2. If the volume of British investment is to be(A) increased, other(B) demands on national resources were having to(C) be reduced or eliminated(D).

3. If traffic problems are not solved soon(A), driving(B) in(C) cities becomes(D) impossible.

4. When he retires(A), Professor Jones will be teaching(B) here for over(C) thirty years, but his classes are(D) never dull.

5. Almost(A) every morning I receive cards inviting(B) me(C) to art exhibitions, and on the cards had been(D) photographs of the works exhibited.

6. Learning a foreign language is especially(A) difficult for those(B) who had(C) never learned one before(D).

7. Although racoons have no special(A) diet, they prefer(B) fish and often became(C) proficient at(D) fishing.

연구 및 정답

1. (D) 시간 부사절에서는 현재시제로 미래를 대신함.
2. (C) 조건문은 is to로 미래(조건)를 표시하였으므로, 주절의 C를 미래형으로 고쳐야 옳음. 그런데 have to의 미래형은 will have to임.
3. (D) 조건 부사절은 현재시제, 주절은 will(미래시제)로.
4. (B) By the time he retires 또는 기간표시 'for'로 보아 B는 미래 완료(진행)형으로 고침.
5. (D) 주절의 시제가 현재이다. had been → are.
6. (C) 주절의 시제가 현재이다. had → have.
7. (C) 본문의 시제가 현재이다. 일반적인 습관을 기술하고 있다. became → become.

Ⅳ. Vocabulary

※ Choose the one which has the closest meaning with the underlined part.

1. The old man scorned whatever was offered to him.
   (A) liked　(B) ate
   (C) rejected　(D) accepted
2. The duration of one cycle of a circadian rhythm is approximately twenty-four hours.
   (A) length　(B) severity
   (C) frequency　(D) penetration
3. The formality of the party made Lucy shy.
   (A) familiarity　(B) shape
   (C) outward from　(D) stiffness of manner
4. The Romantics did not simply repudiate the faith in reasons.
   (A) blame　(B) reject
   (C) imitate　(D) discern
5. Many pure metals have little use because they are too soft, rust to easily, or have some other drawback.
   (A) property　(B) additive
   (C) disadvantage　(D) disparity
6. The child's misdemeanour was never taken seriously by his parents.
   (A) periods of sickness　(B) wrong doings
   (C) rude words　(D) mistakes
7. There was a profound silence in the empty church.
   (A) peculiar　(B) unexpected
   (C) long　(D) deep

연구

1. scorn 경멸하다, 거절하다.
2. duration 기간.
3. formality 형식에 구애됨, 딱딱함.
4. repudiate 거절하다.
5. drawback 결점, 결함.
6. misdemeanour 경범죄, 나쁜 행실.
7. profound 깊은, 심오한. peculiar 독특한, 묘한.

정답

1. C　2. A　3. D　4. B　5. C　6. B　7. D

1. I have no recollection of that incident.
(A) idea (B) opinion
(C) need (D) memory

2. The check was marked void.
(A) insufficient (B) canceled
(C) valid (D) payable

3. That manufacturing method is obsolete.
(A) archaic (B) out-of-date
(C) dilapidated (D) extant

4. That accounts for his gloomy looking.
(A) counts (B) concerns
(C) explains (D) means

5. It's impolite to break in when someone else is talking.
(A) invade (B) destroy
(C) interrupt (D) make noises

6. The surface of the lake was placid.
(A) unruffled (B) colored
(C) solid (D) pleasant to see

7. He was thoughtful for a while and then cried.
(A) fanciful (B) pensive
(C) lustful (D) obstinate

연구

1. recollection 기억.
2. void 무효의, 취소된.
3. obsolete 케케묵은.
4. account for 설명하다.
5. break in 간섭하다, 끼어들다.
6. placid 평온한.
7. thoughtful 생각이 깊은.

정답

1. D 2. B 3. B 4. C 5. C 6. A 7. B

CHAPTER 3

NOUN

I. Grammar Focus

A. 명사의 종류

Once there was **a wise king** named Solomon. (보통)

The committee is made up of 12 members. (집합)

She likes **coffee** very much. (물질)

Albert Einstein was born in Germany. (고유)

Happiness consists in contentment. (추상)

1. 보통명사

A dog (= **The dog**) is a faithful animal. (대표단수)

The pen is mightier than **the sword**. (추상명사화)

All the village were delighted at the news. (all 지명: 사는 사람들)

He lives in **a palace of a house**. (~와 같은)

2. 집합명사

(1) Police형 (사회의 계층) :

반드시 the를 사용하며 복수로 취급(police, peasantry, nobility…)

The police are searching for the missing child.

(2) Cattle형 (단순한 무리) :

the를 사용하지 않으며 복수로 취급(cattle, poultry, fish, people)

Cattle feed on grass.

(3) Family형 (사회의 조직) :

[전체로 보는 관점 : 단수
  구성원 중심의 관점(군집) : 복수(family, committee, audience, class, crowd, jury)

My family are all early risers.

The committee deals with its project.

(4) Furniture형 (집합 +물질명사) :

양으로 다루고, 부정관사 사용 못하며 항상 단수형으로 사용(furniture, stationery, machinery, luggage, merchandise, produce, game, poetry, clothing)

There is **little furniture** in her room.

A table is **a piece of furniture.**

3. 추상명사

She was **kindness itself.** (강조용법)

You should have respect for **age.** (집합명사화)

He had **the kindness** to show me the way. (kindly)

A man **of learning** is not always a man **of wisdom.** (of 추상명사 : 형용사구)

Key Point

have the 추상명사 용법 「~할 정도로 (추상명사) 하다」

have the kindness to (do) = kindly (do)

He **had the kindness to** show me the way.

= He was so kind as to show me the way.

= He **was kind enough to** show me the way.

= He **kindly** showed me the way.

(그는 고맙게도 내게 길을 안내해 주었다.)

4. 물질명사 · 추상명사의 수 표시

Give me **a cup of** coffee.

Could you bring me **a glass of** beer? (물질명사)

Let me give you **a piece of** advice.

That's **a useful piece of** information. (추상명사)

물질 · 추상명사는 수표시를 하는데 있어 "기수+단위명사+of" (조수사)를 사용한다.

※ 물질명사의 단위 표시

a slice of bread (cake, meat) 「한 조각의 빵(케이크, 고기)」

a strip of cloth (land) 「(기다란) 한 조각의 천(땅)」

a grain of rice (corn) 「한 알의 쌀(옥수수)」

an ear of corn 「옥수수 한 개」

a spoonful of sugar 「한 숟갈의 설탕」

※ 추상명사의 단위 표시

a piece of good luck(folly) 「한 차례의 행운(어리석은 짓)」

some bits of scandal(information, news) 「몇 가지의 추문(소식, 뉴스)」

several cases of theft(malaria, typhoid) 「몇 건의 도둑질(말라리아 환자, 장티프스)」

a fit of fever(anger, hysteria) 「한 차례의 (발작적인)고열 (분노, 히스테리)」

※ 중요한 불가산 명사들

equipment, furniture, money, advice, information, baggage/luggage, scenery, news, mail

5. 명사의 전용

(1) 보통명사→추상명사

the mother : 모정, the father : 부정

the poet : 시흥, the novelist : 소설가적 자질

the cradle : 어린 시절, the grave : 죽을 때

the head : 지력, the heart : 심정

(2) 고유명사→보통명사

He wants to be **a Picaso**. (~의 특징이 있는 사람)

There are **three Kims** in our club. (~라는 이름을 가진 사람)

The Smiths are an old family. (~가의 사람들)

The museum has **three Millets and two Picassos**. (작품이름)

(3) 물질명사→보통명사

Many different **whiskies** are produced in Scotland. (종류)

He threw **a stone** into the river. (개체)

There are **two irons** and **three glasses** on the table. (제품)

(4) 추상명사→보통명사

She showed me **a kindness** at the party. (행동)

My mother was **a beauty** in her day. (특징을 가진 사람)

Modesty is **a virtue**. (특징)

B. 주의해야 할 복수의 유형

1. 상시복수 (항상 복수로 쓰이는 명사)

(짝을 이루는) : 복수로 취급(scissors, trousers, socks, stockings, shoes, glasses)

(-ic학문명, 병명) : 단수로 취급(mathematics, physics, ethics, measles, blues)

My trousers are laid on the bed.

A pair of shoes is bought at the store.

Physics is my major field.

2. 분화복수(단수 · 복수의 의미가 다른 명사)

air(공기) airs(으시대는 태도)	arm(팔) arms(무기)	pain(고통) pains(수고)	number(수) numbers(운문)
custom(관습) customs(관세)	content(만족) contents(내용)	work(일) works(공장)	ruin(파멸) ruins(폐허)
force(힘) forces(군대)	good(선; 이익) goods(상품)	color(색) colors(군기)	advice(충고) advices(외교·정치상의 보고)
letter(편지; 문자) letters(문학)	manner(방법; 태도) manners(예절)	provision(설비) provisions(양식)	
quarter(1/4) quarters(숙소, 막사)	part(부분) parts(재능)	spirit(정신) spirits(원기)	

3. 상호복수 (서로의 관계표시로 항상 복수사용)

be on good **terms** with : 사이가 좋다.

change **cars** : 차를 바꾸어 타다.

take **turns** : 교대하다.

exchange **seats** with : 자리를 교환하다.

make **friends** with : 친구를 사귀다.

shake **hands** with : 악수하다.

4. 「짜리~」의 의미전달

기수-단위명사(단수)+명사

기수-단위명사(복수)+형용사(부사)

기수-단위명사(단수)=형용사+명사

a five-**dollar** bill

a ten-**mile** race

a ten-**year**-old boy

a five-**year**-economic development plan

three **inches** thick

five **feet** long

5. 가격, 시간, 거리, 중량의 명사는 복수형이라도 하나의 단위취급으로 단수사용

Ten **years** is a long time to wait.

Ten **years** have passed since he died.

(동사 pass와 결합 시 단일개념으로 간주 할 수 없음, 복수 취급)

Five **miles** is too long to walk.

Three **dollars** is all I need.

C. 명사의 격

생물의 소유격은 's를 취하고, 무생물의 소유격은 of+N 형태를 취한다.

예외1. 원칙은 무생물명사의 소유격은 "of-소유격"을 사용하나 다음과 같은 경우는 "-s"를 사용한다.

• 의인화된 무생물

Korea's foreign trade(한국의 해외 무역), the sun's rays(태양 광선)

the **earth**'s surface(지구 표면), the world's history(=the history of the world)

• 시간을 나타내는 명사

Where is **today**'s paper?

He came home after three **years**' **absence**.

• 거리·중량·가격을 나타내는 명사

He lives at a **stone**'s throw from here.

Give me a **pound**'s weight of sugar.

• 관용구

He is **at his wit's end** what to do. (당황하다)

I enjoyed skiing **to my heart's content.** (실컷)

He knows it **at his finger's ends.** (익숙한)

Spare me **for mercy's sake.** (제발)

예외2. 독립소유격 (소유격만 사용하고 명사는 생략)

(소유격) John's mother is older than **Mary's (mother).**

That's my fault, not **my brother's (fault).**

I have stayed at **my uncle's (house).**

(소유격) the **doctor's (office)**

St. **Paul's (cathedral)**

예외3. 이중소유격(of 명사's) 용법

한정사(this, that, which, what, some, any, a(n), no, another) + 명사일 경우 이중소유격 사용

I met **a friend of Mary's.**

This book of Hemingway's is interesting.

No friend of John's attended the party.

D. 명사의 성

1. 성의 구별이 있는 명사

(a) host↔hostess, heir↔heiress, hero↔heroine

(b) boy-student↔girl-student, he-goat↔she-goat

(c) nephew↔niece, king↔queen, widower↔widow, bridegroom↔bride, monk↔nun, bachelor↔spinster, cock↔hen, horse↔mare, etc.

2. 의인화된 명사

남성 취급(he) : 강렬함, 맹렬함, 위대함, 두려움, 잔인성을 나타내는 것
sun, winter, river, ocean, death, war, cruelty, love, time, etc.

여성 취급(she) : 아름다움, 우아함, 평화로움, 약함, 온순함을 나타내는 것
spring, moon, nature, earth, peace, mercy, art, etc.

3. 배, 열차, 비행기는 여성으로 받는 것이 보통이다.

The ship sank with all **her** crew.

4. 국가명은 정치, 경제면에 대해서는 여성으로 받고 지리적(국토)일 때는 it(중성)으로 받는다.(아이도 중성)

England is proud of **her** great poets.

Korea is famous for **its** scenery.

E. 명사의 일치

1. There(Here)로 시작되는 구문은 그 다음 명사에 의해 동사의 수 결정

There **are several ways** to solve the problem.

There **is a boy** in the garden.

2. A and B 구문

Curry and rice **is** my favorite food.(단일 개념)

Tom and Mary **are** roommates this semester.

3. 관사+A and B ⇒단수, 관사 A and 관사 B ⇒복수

A black and white dog **is** barking at a stranger.

A black and a white dog **are** barking at a stranger.

4. 시간, 거리, 가격, 무게 등은 단수로 받는다.

Ten years **is** a long time to wait alone. (시간)

Forty miles **is** a long distance. (거리)

Fifty dollars **is** too much to pay that coat. (가격)

Two hundred pounds **is** a big burden for me to bear. (무게)

5. 병명, 학과명, 운동명, 복수의 국가명, news 등은 단수로 받는다.

Measles **is** dreadful.(병명)

Linguistics **is** his strong point.(학과명)

Billiards **is** usually played by two persons.(운동명)

The United States **is** a big country.(국가명)

6. 집합명사 (전체 : 단수, 개체 : 복수)

종류 – family, class, committee, crew, audience

The committee **consists of** twelve person. (집합명사)

The committee **are divided in** their opinions. (군집명사)

7. 근접원리법(근접에 있는 명사에 수를 일치시키는 법칙)

A or B
either A or B
neither A nor B
not only A but also B

\+ V (B에 의해서 수 결정)

ex) Either he or **you are** going to help me.

8.

The number of +단(복)수명사+단수동사
A number of + 복수명사+복수동사

Many a+단수명사+단수동사
Many+복수명사+복수동사

More than+단수명사+단수동사
More than+복수명사+복수동사

9. 분수(부분)

The rest
Part
All + of + **정해진 명사** + 동사
Half
Most

ex) The rest of the apple is rotten.

The rest of the apples are rotten.

10.

Every(one, body, thing)
Any(one, body, thing)
No(one, body, thing) + 단수동사
Either
Neither

Anybody who has lost his ID card should report th the office.

11.

A [accompanied by / along with / in addition to / as well as / together with / no less than] B+V (동사의 수는 A에 의해 결정)

Tom, accompanied by his wife and children, is arriving here.

F. 명사에서 주의해야 할 부분

① 명사+명사의 경우

book store(책방)의 경우에서 book이 비록 명사이지만 store를 수식하는 형용사 역할을 하기 때문에 book에 -s를 붙일 수 없다.

② a four-year-old girl에서 year 다음에 -s를 붙일 수 없다.

그 이유는 four-year-old가 girl을 수식하는 형용사 성질을 띠기 때문에, 형용사에는 -s를 붙일 수 없다.

③ ten, hundred, thousand, million 앞에 수사가 있으면 이들 단어 다음 -s를 붙이지 못하지만 이들 단어 앞에 수사가 없이 막연한 수사를 나타내는 경우에 이들 단어 다음에 -s를 붙이고 of+복수명사의 형태를 취한다.

ex) 2천명(two thousands→ two thousand)

수십 명(ten people→ tens of people)

④ 명사+기수=the+서수+명사

Lesson ten=the tenth Lesson

(page, war, chapter 등)

단, Track two(O)=the second Track(X), Gate two(O)=the second Gate(X)

(window, lane, car 등)

II. Sentence Structure

1. She was in _____ when she got married.
   (A) thirty's (B) her thirties
   (C) the thirties (D) her thirty

2. I was at my _____ end to answer the question.
   (A) wit's (B) sake's
   (C) hand's (D) wisdom's

3. She must be near-sighted, for she wears _____.
   (A) a spectacle (B) spectacles
   (C) a glass of spectacle (D) a pair of spectacles

4. She arrived here with _____.
   (A) some baggages (B) a few baggage
   (C) much baggage (D) lots of baggages

5. He showed me _____ a few days ago.
   (A) some his father's books (B) his father's some books
   (C) his father's books of some (D) some books of his father's

6. The audience _____ by his speech.
   (A) were moved (B) was moved
   (C) moved (D) moves

7. He felt _____ rise in him at the news.
   (A) a patriot (B) patriot
   (C) one patriot (D) the patriot

연구 및 정답

1. (B) 몇 십대의 표현.
2. (A) at one's wit's end 어쩔 줄 모르는.
3. (D) 안경 등은 쌍으로 복수 표시.
4. (C) baggage, luggage는 불가산 명사.
5. (D) 이중소유격.
6. (A) 군중은 군집명사로 복수취급.
7. (D) the+단수보통명사: 추상명사(patriotism 애국심).

1. _____ of job performance usually takes place at the end of the week.
   (A) Reviewed (B) Reviewer
   (C) Review (D) Reviews

2. The company received numerous _____ about the quality of products.
   (A) complaining (B) complains
   (C) complaints (D) to complain

3. The company accepted _____ for those defective products.
   (A) responsibility (B) responsible
   (C) response (D) to response

4. The store on the first floor of the hotel sells a _____ of souvenirs.
   (A) various (B) variety
   (C) vary (D) varying

5. Employees in the payroll department gave their _____ to the charity last week.
   (A) donate (B) donations
   (C) donator (D) to donate

6. We tried to handle the fragile items with _____ when they were delivered.
   (A) cautious (B) caution
   (C) cautiously (D) cautioned

7. We really would like to get _____ about the traffic accident.
   (A) some information (B) an information
   (C) informations (D) plenty of informations

연구 및 정답

1. (C) 업무실적 평가.
2. (C) 형용사 + 명사.
3. (A) 타동사의 목적어 필요.
4. (B) a variety of: 다양한.
5. (B) 기부금 표현은?
6. (B) 전치사 + 명사: 전명구는 형용사 혹은 부사 기능.
7. (A) information은 불가산 명사임.

1. Customer _____ is important to stay competitive in the global market.
   (A) success (B) loyal
   (C) satisfaction (D) greatness

2. _____ received after December 10 will be sent back to the applicants.
   (A) Applicable (B) Applied
   (C) Applicants (D) Applications

3. If you don't have a parking permit, your car may be towed at your _____.
   (A) expense (B) fee
   (C) fare (D) charge

4. Many firms relieve security concerns with the use of high tech _____ devices.
   (A) secure (B) securely
   (C) secured (D) security

5. I cut ten _____.
   (A) slice of bread (B) slices of bread
   (C) slices of breads (D) slice of breads

6. I met a lot of _____ at the party.
   (A) peoples (B) people
   (C) person (D) a person

7. _____ is good for you.
   (A) Jogging (B) Jogs
   (C) To jogging (D) Jog

연구 및 정답

1. (C) 고객 만족의 표현은?
2. (D) 주어로 서류들이란 표현은?
3. (A) at one's expense: 그 대가로.
4. (D) 안전장치.
5. (B) bread는 물질명사이므로 불가산 명사.
6. (B) 사람들이란 표현으로 알맞은 것은?
7. (A) 주어로는 명사류가 답이다.

Ⅲ. Grammar Practice

1. There <u>are</u> eleven <u>player</u> <u>on</u> <u>a</u> soccer team.
   A B C D

2. Every <u>countries</u> uses <u>stamps</u> and <u>many</u> people <u>collect</u> them.
   A B C D

3. <u>The</u> tallest <u>building</u> in the US is the Sears Tower in Chicago, and <u>it's</u> 1,454 <u>foots</u> tall.
   A B C D

4. <u>These</u> days many <u>woman</u> work <u>after</u> they <u>marry</u>.
   A B C D

5. We <u>call</u> a person a <u>musicians</u> <u>if</u> he or she <u>makes</u> songs and sings songs.
   A B C D

6. <u>People</u> eat <u>a lot</u> of <u>potato</u> in <u>this</u> country.
   A B C D

7. <u>Anyone</u> over sixteen can <u>get</u> a driver's <u>licenses</u> in <u>the United States</u>.
   A B C D

연구 및 정답

1. (B) eleven 복수가산명사.
2. (A) every, each 다음에는 단수 가산명사가 답이다.
3. (D) foot의 복수형은?
4. (B) woman의 복수 형태는?
5. (B) a(n) + 단수가산명사.
6. (C) a lot of 다음에는 복수가산, 불가산 명사 다 올 수 있다.
7. (C) a(n) + 단수가산명사.

1. Mathematic (A) and logic depend extensively (B) on the deductive (C) method of reasoning (D).

2. The valerian family includes (A) more (B) than 300 different kinds of perennial or annual (C) herb (D) and a few shrubs.

3. Economists study the relationship between the number (A) of money in (B) circulation and the number (C) of goods being produced (D).

4. People has (A) always felt the need (B) to express themselves (C) through (D) movement.

5. Sunlights (A) cannot reach (B) far beneath (C) the ocean's surface (D).

6. It was during the 1920's that (A) the friendship between (B) Hemingway and Fitzgerald reached their (C) highest (D) point.

7. The spectators were (A) dispersed by (B) the police who was (C) at the scene (D).

연구 및 정답

1. (A) Mathematic은 형용사이므로 명사인 logic과 더불어 본문의 주어가 될 수 없다. 따라서 명사인 Mathematics로 고친다.
2. (D) herb는 가산명사이다. kinds of + 복수명사. herb → herbs.
3. (A) money가 셀 수 없는 명사임에 착안할 것. the number → the amount.
4. (A) people은 복수명사이다. has → have.
5. (A) Sunlight는 추상명사이다. Sunlights → Sunlight.
6. (C) the friendship은 추상명사, 단수로 받음.
7. (C) the police는 복수취급.

Ⅳ. Vocabulary

※ Choose the one which has the closest meaning with the underlined part.

1. Don't bother me with <u>trivial</u> matter.
   (A) troublesome (B) mutual
   (C) not important (D) significant
2. Cheese is made by <u>allowing</u> milk to ripen or age.
   (A) forcing (B) permitting
   (C) expecting (D) mixing
3. It is a new kind of metal <u>able to bend</u> without breaking.
   (A) speculative (B) flexible
   (C) irresistible (D) amiable
4. This tapestry has a very <u>complicated</u> pattern.
   (A) obsolete (B) ultimate
   (C) antique (D) intricate
5. I cannot <u>endure</u> this toothache any longer.
   (A) endow with (B) go with
   (C) put up with (D) anger with
6. He <u>criticized</u> the woman.
   (A) do away with (B) found fault with
   (C) turned down (D) stood for
7. <u>Motivation</u> is a primary factor in learning.
   (A) Intelligence (B) Incentive
   (C) Aptitude (D) Memorization

연구

1. trivial 하찮은, 사소한(=insignificant=trifling)
2. allow 허용하다(=permit)
3. bend 구부리다, 휘다.
4. complicated 복잡한(=intricate, complex)
5. endure 참다, 견디다(tolerate, bear, stand, put up with)
6. criticize ~을 비판하다, 욕하다(=find fault with)
7. incentive 동기, 자극. aptitude 적응성, 소질.

정답

1. C 2. B 3. B 4. D 5. C 6. B 7. B

1. Potential computer buyers have come to expect versatility, energy efficiency, and simplicity, as <u>essential</u> components of new equipment.
   (A) necessary (B) nominal
   (C) suspicious (D) tangible

2. <u>Experts</u> note that a child acquires language spontaneously, without systematic instruction.
   (A) Authorities (B) Observers
   (C) Parents (D) Administration

3. Ice skates manufactured <u>entirely</u> of iron were first sold in the 1800's.
   (A) mainly (B) successfully
   (C) solely (D) routinely

4. The mammalian respiratory system depends on the functioning of an <u>energetic</u> heart and extremely absorptive blood.
   (A) elastic (B) enlarged
   (C) vigorous (D) specialized

5. Ralph Bunche won a Nobel Prize in 1950 for his peacemaking <u>efforts</u> as a United Nations diplomat.
   (A) requests (B) attempts
   (C) offers (D) trips

6. Settings and costumes are not <u>extraneous</u> accessories, but rather constituents of the ballet's expressive medium.
   (A) unessential (B) costly
   (C) marvelous (D) aesthetic

7. As photographic techniques have become more sophisticated, the scope of their application has expanded <u>enormously</u>.
   (A) diversely (B) flagrantly
   (C) appealingly (D) tremendously

연구

1. essential: needed, necessary, important, vital.
2. expert: skill, clever, master, authority.
3. entirely: completely, wholly, solely, totally.
4. energy: force, strength, vigor, vitality.
5. effort: attempt, try, endeavor.
6. extraneous: foreign, unrelated, unessential.
7. enormous: vast, immense, huge, colossal, giant.

정답

1. A 2. A 3. C 4. C 5. B 6. A 7. D

CHAPTER 4

PRONOUN

I. Grammar Focus

대명사의 종류: 인칭대명사, 지시대명사, 의문대명사, 부정대명사, 관계대명사

A. 인칭대명사

1. we, they, you : 막연한 일반인을 표시

They say that he is honest.

We are often blind to our own faults.

2. it가 비인칭 대명사로 쓰일 때

(1) 날씨, 명암, 시간 , 거리, 계절을 나타낼 때

It is fine today. It is spring now.

(2) 막연한 상황을 나타낼 때

How goes **it** with you? How is **it** in the market?

3. It ~ that 강조 구문

(1) 평서문의 강조

I bought the book yesterday.

→ **It was** I **that**(who) bought the book yesterday. (I를 강조)

(2) 의문문의 강조

Did you send me the flower? →You sent me the flower.

→ **It was you that** sent me the flower →**Was it you that** sent me the flower?

B. 소유대명사

1. 소유격+명사 = 소유대명사

This dictionary is mine(=my dictionary).

2. 이중소유격

소유격은 a(n), no, this, that, another 등과 나란히 쓸 수 없으며 of+소유대명사의 형태로 쓴다.

her a (this, another) book (X)

a(this another) book of hers (O)

C. 재귀대명사

① 재귀용법 : 타동사나 전치사의 목적어로써 쓰인 경우(생략 불가능)

He always prides himself on his son.

We enjoyed ourselves at the party.

② 강조용법 : 주어나 목적어의 동격이 되어 그것의 뜻을 강조한다. (생략 가능)

You must take care of it **yourself.**

The matter itself is an unsolved mystery.

③ 관용적용법 : 전치사+재귀대명사

by oneself (=alone : 홀로)

for oneself (=without others help : 혼자 힘으로)

beside oneself (=almost mad, insane : 제 정신이 아닌)

of oneself (=spontaneously, automatically : 저절로)

in itself (=naturally : 본질적으로)

in spite of oneself (자기도 모르게)

D. 지시대명사

1. This/that

① To be or not to be; **that** is the question.

② The climate of Busan is milder than **that**(=the climate) of Seoul.

③ Work and play are both necessary to health : **this**(=play) gives us rest, and **that**(=work) gives us energy.

④ It rained, and **that** in torrents.

Key Point

① this/that : 앞(또는 뒤)에 나온 문장이나 어구를 대신할 수 있다.
This is my philosophy: think today and speak tomorrow.

② that of~, those of~: 앞에 나온 명사의 반복을 피하기 위해 쓰며, 반복되는 명사가 단수이면 that, 복수이면 those를 쓴다.
His manners are **those** of a little boy. (those=the manners)

③ this 후자(가까운 것)that 전자(먼 것)
the former, the one (전자) the latter, the other (후자)

④ and that (그것도~)
You must go, and that at once.

2. so, such, the same

(1) so의 용법

동사 think, suppose, say, hope, do 다음에 와서 앞 문장 전체 또는 일부를 대신한다.

So 주어 동사 (certainly, indeed 사실, 정말)

So 동사 주어 (also, too ~도 역시)

I hear he is very rich. So he is.

(2) such의 용법

앞에 나온 명사 또는 앞 문장 전체를 받는다.

He was shot dead. **Such** was the way of God.

(3) the same의 용법

① 동일물, 동일인의 표시

She called for **the same** again.

② the same as + 명사 : ~와 같은(부사)

My opinion is **the same as** yours.

③ all the same: 그래도 역시(nevertheless)

He has some defects, but I like him **all the same**.

F. 부정대명사

1. one

- a+명사 - one
- the 명사 - it

두 개 있을 때: one, the other

세 개 있을 때: one, another, the third

네 개 있을 때: one, another, a third, the fourth

열 개 있을 때: some(4), the others(6)

열 개 있을 때: some(3), others(5)

(1) one으로 받을 수 없는 명사

불가산 명사

John liked red wine better than white one. (X)

own 다음

He has a car. So he wants to use his own one. (X)

수사 다음

He has three cars and I have two ones. (X)

(2) A is one thing~B is another A와B는 별개의 것이다.

To know is one thing, and to teach is another.

2. some, any

some : 긍정문 (단, yes의 답을 기대할 때나 권유나 의뢰를 나타낼 때는 의문문에도 some을 쓴다.)

any : 부정문, 의문문, 조건문 (단 해석이 어떤~라도 라고 해석될 때는 긍정문에서도 any를 쓴다.)

3. no, not, none

no : 명사 부정 (형용사)

not : 동사부정 (부사)

none : 대명사로 쓰임 (no one)

4. either, neither

either, neither 다음에는 단수 취급한다.

either : 둘 중의 하나

any : 셋 이상

5. 부분 부정

not+(always, entirely, every, both, all)

완전부정

(not – in the least, not at all, never)

II. Sentence Structure

1. Have you seen _____ stapler?
   (A) I'm (B) my
   (C) mine (D) me

2. I can do my homework by _____.
   (A) mine (B) me
   (C) myself (D) my

3. After you collect the money, you need to count _____.
   (A) it (B) them
   (C) they (D) anything

4. There are two balls in the box. One is white and _____ is blue and red.
   (A) other (B) others
   (C) the other (D) the others

5. All of us would like to show _____ special thanks for your help.
   (A) ours (B) us
   (C) ourselves (D) our

6. Linda convinced _____ boss to accept the offer.
   (A) hers (B) her
   (C) she (D) herself

7. The sales manager _____ admitted that sales would go down soon.
   (A) his (B) him
   (C) he (D) himself

연구 및 정답

1. (B) 소유격 + 명사.
2. (C) by oneself: alone 혼자서.
3. (A) the money를 받는 대명사는?
4. (C) 둘 중 하나는 one 다른 하나는 the other.
5. (D) 소유격 + 형용사 + 명사.
6. (B) 소유격 + 명사.
7. (D) 완전한 문장. 강조 용법의 재귀대명사.

1. _____ of the clerks was instructed to do his own work.
   (A) Every (B) Each
   (C) Some (D) Most

2. _____ but peace can save the world.
   (A) Anything (B) Something
   (C) Nothing (D) Anyone

3. The door opened _____.
   (A) for itself (B) by itself
   (C) of itself (D) in itself

4. I don't like this. Please show me _____.
   (A) the other (B) other
   (C) some (D) another

5. Some people like fishing; _____ do not.
   (A) others (B) the other
   (C) the others (D) another

6. Most _____ work hard.
   (A) of employees (B) employees
   (C) employee (D) of employee

7. _____ in this department was busy preparing for the conference last week.
   (A) Every person (B) Every people
   (C) All people (D) All the people

연구 및 정답

1. (B) his로 보아 단수 취급하는 걸 받는 것이 정답.
2. (C) nothing but: only.
3. (C) 저절로의 올바른 표현은?
4. (D) a different thing: another.
5. (A) some ~ others vs some ~ the others.
6. (B) Most of the employees; Most employees.
7. (A) Every + 단수명사 + 단수동사.

1. Every culture _____ styles and traditions of singing.
   (A) has its own (B) have its own
   (C) has their own (D) have their own

2. I have three brothers, _____ is a doctor, _____ a teacher, and the third a businessman.
   (A) one - other (B) one - another
   (C) one - the other (D) the one - the other

3. All of you should think long and hard about _____ before choosing a job.
   (A) you (B) your
   (C) yours (D) yourselves

4. The team is preparing for _____.
   (A) its big game (B) it's big game
   (C) their big game (D) theirs big game

5. Students should do _____.
   (A) his best (B) your best
   (C) our best (D) their best

6. The president hopes that you will call _____ immediately to let him know about the results.
   (A) himself (B) he
   (C) him (D) his

7. Mr. Admin and Ms. Tota devised innovative strategies and _____ proved to be useful.
   (A) we (B) themselves
   (C) they (D) us

연구 및 정답

1. (A) every는 모든 단수 명사, 단수동사와 어울림.
2. (B) 세 명 표시는 one ~ another ~ the other(the third).
3. (D) 너희들을 받는 재귀대명사는?
4. (A) 그것의 소유격은?
5. (D) 학생들의 소유격은?
6. (C) call의 목적어 필요.
7. (C) 동사 prove를 볼 때 주격인 they가 정답.

Ⅲ. Grammar Practice

1. American(A) people liked(B) John F. Kennedy because they(C) had new ideas(D).

2. Many(A) plants make(B) flowers and their(C) make seeds(D).

3. Alexander Graham Bell and their(A) assistant Watson tried(B) to send(C) speech through(D) a wire.

4. When(A) letters are(B) big, we(C) call they(D) capital letters.

5. Since(A) its(B) is a northern(C) country, Canada is cold in(D) the winter.

6. Birds(A) spend much(B) of its(C) time in(D) the air.

7. When a character(A) is a girl or(B) woman, we call(C) it(D) a heroine.

연구 및 정답

1. (C) Kennedy를 받는 대명사는?
2. (C) 주어의 형태는?
3. (A) 3인칭 단수의 소유격은?
4. (D) 3인칭 복수의 목적격 형태.
5. (B) 국가를 나타내는 3인칭 단수 주어.
6. (C) 3인칭 복수명사의 소유격 표시.
7. (D) 여성을 받는 목적격 형태는?

1. When Amundsen made (A) his plan to sail to the (B) Arctic, she (C) spent a lot of (D) money getting ready and owed money to many people.

2. All the (A) students are working (B) late (C) tonight to finish his (D) reports.

3. If a person really wants (A) to succeed, it (B) should always (C) work hard (D).

4. All living (A) creatures pass on (B) inherited traits from (C) one generation to other (D).

5. When I lost my (A) passport, I had to (B) apply the (C) another one (D).

6. Rachel and her (A) husband have known (B) one after another (C) since they were (D) children.

7. In 1947 (A), India gained their (B) independence from Britain (C), but the country was split (D) into mainly Hindu India and mainly Muslim Pakistan.

연구 및 정답

1. (C) Amundsen은 남성명사임.
2. (D) students는 복수명사이므로 소유격은?
3. (B) a person을 받는 대명사는?
4. (D) from one generation to another (generation).
5. (C) the와 another같이 쓸 수 없음.
6. (C) each other(둘 사이 서로), one after another(셋 이상 서로).
7. (B) 국가의 소유격은? 정치적인 부분은 her임.

Ⅳ. Vocabulary

※ Choose the one which has the closest meaning with the underlined part.

1. An advantage of a democracy is that we can amend our laws when necessary.
   (A) make (B) impair
   (C) reform (D) corrupt

2. The motorcycle police preceded the president's car to clear a path.
   (A) followed (B) went before
   (C) traveled with (D) keep up with

3. He tried every means to get the better of his rival, but in vain.
   (A) get the worse of (B) win
   (C) get away (D) get at

4. This list must be learned by heart.
   (A) grasped fully (B) observed faithfully
   (C) memorized (D) believed

5. Her bright brown hair made her stand out from the others.
   (A) separate (B) insult
   (C) isolate (D) distinguish

6. We had to call off our plan because it rained cats and dogs.
   (A) postpone (B) cancel
   (C) examine (D) criticize

7. I understand the factory is going to lay off a hundred men this month.
   (A) call back (B) dismiss temporarily
   (C) give the leave (D) employ

연구

1. amend 개정하다.
2. precede 선행하다, 앞서 가다.
3. get the better of 이기다.
4. learned by heart 암기하다.
5. stand out 두드러지다.
6. call off 취소하다.
7. lay off 해고하다.

정답

1. C 2. B 3. B 4. C 5. D 6. B 7. B

1. Molly Brown was labeled "unsinkable" after she helped to <u>evacuate</u> passengers from the ill-fated ship the Titanic.
   (A) anticipate (B) comfort
   (C) remove (D) shelter

2. After its founding, the United States government followed a policy <u>explicitly</u> designed to aid national shipping.
   (A) prematurely (B) economically
   (C) specifically (D) proudly

3. Biomedical research may soon discover a way to <u>extend</u> human life.
   (A) improve (B) duplicate
   (C) change (D) lengthen

4. Horseback riding <u>embraces</u> both the skill of handing a horse and mastery of diverse riding styles.
   (A) fosters (B) emphasizes
   (C) exaggerates (D) includes

5. Ella Grasso, elected governor of Connecticut in 1974, supported the <u>enactment</u> of a freedom-of-information law.
   (A) passing (B) advocate
   (C) drafting (D) circulation

6. Flatworms <u>evolved</u> over 600 million years ago.
   (A) developed (B) rotated
   (C) escaped (D) shrank

7. Theories about the existence and location of the lost continent of Atlantis have always generated conjecture and <u>enthusiasm</u> among archaeologists.
   (A) apprehension (B) jealousy
   (C) intense interest (D) great hostility

연구

1. evacuate: withdraw, remove, deprive, leave.
2. explicit: clear, distinct, definite, candid.
3. extend: lengthen, stretch, increase, escalate
4. embrace: contain, include, comprehend, comprise.
5. enact: pass, legislate.
6. evolve: unfold, develop, grow, progress.
7. enthusiasm: eagerness, warmth, zeal, ardor.

정답

1. C 2. C 3. D 4. D 5. C 6. A 7. C

CHAPTER 5

ADJECTIVE

I. Grammar Focus

A. 형용사의 용법

It is an **interesting** book.

She was in a **woolen** suit of pale yellow. (한정적 용법)

The book is **interesting**.

He was **awake** all the night. (서술적 용법)

A **certain** young man told me so.

It is **certain** that two and two make four. (의미가 달라지는 형용사)

1. 한정적 용법

명사를 직접 수식하는 형용사(woolen, wooden, golden, drunken, elder, former, latter, outer, upper, utmost...)

That man is an **utter** fool.

She was combing her **golden** hair.

2. 서술적 용법

보어로서 설명하는 형용사(awake, asleep, alive, afraid, alike, content, unable, worth, glad, sorry...)

I am not **alone** in this opinion.

No two children can look exact.

3. 의미가 달라지는 형용사

The **late** Dr. Smith is his nephew. (고인의)

She was **late**. (늦은)

The **present** chairman is Tom. (현재의)

He was **present**. (참석한)

B. 형용사의 위치, 어순

A dictionary **useful** for us.

He is the greatest artist **imaginable**.

She is a lady **beautiful, kind** and **simple**.

Please give me **something** hot.

The two typical large country houses are my bother's.

The five large blue shoes are mine.

1. 형용사의 위치

형용사는 명사 앞에서 원칙으로 수식하나, 다음과 같은 경우는 명사 뒤에서 수식한다.

(1) (최상급, every, all등의 한정어를 수식할 때)

She used all means **imaginable**.

This is the best method **practicable**.

(2) 형용사가 길 때

That is a building **fifty feet high and expansive**.

I met a gentleman **tall, handsome**, and **refined**.

(3) ~thing, ~body를 수식할 때

There is nothing **particular**.

I saw somebody **strange** here.

2. 형용사의 어순

여러 개의 형용사가 겹칠 때는 다음과 같은 어순으로 정리

→ 지시, 수량, 대소, 성질, 상태, 신구, 국적, 재료, + 명사

She read **all these five thick books** in a week.

That large white new wooden house has just been sold.

I happened to meet **these two fine good-natured old English gentle men.**

C. 수량형용사

Quite a few married women go out to work today.

I have only **a few** friends.

Clearing the back yard needed **quite a little** work.

He has **only a little** sense.

Many a man would welcome the opportunity.

It wasn't **much of** a dinner. (not much of a~=not a good)

I didn't **make much** of his work. (~을 중히 여기다)

1. few, little 용법

quite a few(little), not a few(little) : 많은
only a few(little), very few(little), but few(little), so few(little) : 극히 적은

Quite a few students waste their time and energy.
There are **not a few pencils** on the desk.

Only **a few people** went on a picnic.
He has very **few books** in his library

2. many, much의 용법

'many +a(n) 단수명사'는 단수로 취급하며, 'a great many + 복수명사'는 복수로 취급한다.

Many a boat has been wrecked here.

A great many boys wish to see the film.

Key Point 1

little이 동사(expect, hope, wish, dream …)을 수식할 경우 순수부정(전혀~하지 않는)의 의미로 사용된다.

I little dreamed that he was a liar.
Little did I dream that he was a liar.

I little expected him to pass the test.
Little did I expect him to pass the test.

Key Point 2

'동수의, 동량의' 용법 : 같은 문장에서 숫자를 반복할 때와 양을 반복할 때.

He has made seven mistakes; in as many lines.
I found six mistakes; in as many lines.
She bought a pound of sugar, and as much flour.

Key Point 3

관용적 용법

He is **little better than** a beggar.(~와 거의 마찬가지인) : as good as
It is **little short of** a miracle. (거의 : almost)
He is **not so much** a scholar as a journalist.
(~라기보다는 차라리 ~이다)
He **cannot so much as** write his own name.
(~조차도 않다 : not even~)

D. 수사

- 567=five hundred and sixty-seven. 1051=one thousand and fifty-one
- 1965=nineteen sixty-five

  cf) 19 = nineteen blank(nineteen or something)

  1908 = nineteen hundred and eight

  August 3rd = (the) third of August

  1/2 = a half, 1/4 = a quarter

  8 3/5 = eight and three-fifths, 1.23=one point two three

Key Point 1

배수를 나타내는 법

기수 times as 원급 as, 기수 times the 명사 of

[This room is half as large as that one.
  This room is half the size of that one.

[Her brother is three times as old as I.
  Her brother is three times the age of me.

Key Point 2

수 단위 명사(dozen, score, hundred, thousand, million, billion)의 용법

구체적인 수 표시 → 기수 + 수 단위명사(단수) : three score, six hundred, five thousand, seven million

막연한 수 표시 → 수 단위명사(복수) of~ : 수십의 dozens of~. 수백의 hundreds of, 수천의 thousands of~

Key Point 3

관용적 표현

Students are rambling **by twos and threes.** (삼삼오오)

She is now **in her forties**, but then she was **in her teens.** (사십대, 십대)

F. 주의할 형용사의 용법

It is **natural** that you should do your duty.

It is **natural** for you to do your duty.

It is **easy** to solve this problem.

This problem is **easy** to solve.

We should be **respectful** toward our seniors.

A man of wisdom is usually respectable.

The population of Seoul is **larger** than that of Busan.

The price of sugar is very **high**.

(1) 진주어로 'for~to부정사'나 that~should가 잘 쓰이는 형용사(desirable, essential, good, important, natural, necessary, regrettable, right ~)

It is **necessary** that the children should obey their parents.

It is **necessary** for the children to obey their parents.

(2) It is 형용사 to부정사에서 가주어 it 대신에 to부정사의 목적어를 주어로 하여도 같은 뜻의 문장이 되는 형용사(difficult, easy, hard, impossible, pleasant, wonderful)

It is **difficult** to master English.

→ English is **difficult** to master.

(3) 같은 명사나 동사에서 온 형용사가 서로 뜻이 다른 것

① continual(practice) 거듭 되풀이 되는

continuous(performance) 중단되지 않고 계속되는

② credible(information) 믿을 만한

credulous(person) 곧잘 남을 믿는

③ desirous(of learning) 바라고 있는

desirable 바람직한

④ economic(policy) 경제(학)의, 경제에 관한

economical(person) 경제적인, 절약하는

⑤ healthful(food) 건강에 좋은

healthy(baby) 건강한

⑥ historic 역사적, 역사상 유명한

historical 역사(학)의

⑦ industrial 산업의

industrious 근면한

⑧ respectable 존경을 받을 만한, 훌륭한

respectful 공손한

respective 각각의

⑨ sensitive(ears) 민감한

sensible(fellow) 감지할 수 있는, 분별력 있는

sensual(pleasures) 관능적인, 육체적인

sensuous(impressions) 감각적인

G. 비교

1. 원급에 의한 비교급

(1) He is **as** busy **as** a bee.(as 원급 as : 같은 정도 표시)

She is **as** wise **as** fair.

(2) Try to speak **as** clearly **as possible**.(관용적 표현)

He is **as** great a poet **as** ever lived.

(3) as ~ as 비교구문의 관용적 표현

Try to speak as clearly as possible. (as you can) (가능한 ~한)

He is as great a poet as ever lived. (최상급의 의미)

He is as brave a man as any(man) in the world. (최상급의 의미)

She is as poor as(poor) can be. (매우~한)

He is **as good as** dead. (=He is almost dead.) (거의)

cf. He is as good as his word. (=He is reliable.)

2. 우등비교의 기본용법

It is **colder** today **than** yesterday.

She is **the elder** of the two.

She is **more** shy **than** unsocial.

The sky grew **darker and darker**.

(1) 양자 간의 비교

- than clause를 수반하는 경우

  Iron is more useful than gold.

  * 어미가 -or로 끝나는 latin계의 비교급에는 than대신에 to를 사용한다.

  This wine is much superior to that in flavor.

- of the two를 수반하는 경우

  The book is the thicker of the two.

  * of the two와 함께 사용되는 형용사의 비교급에는 정관사를 붙인다.

(2) 동일인, 동일물의 두 가지 다른 성질을 비교할 때

원급의 앞에 more를 사용하여 rather의 뜻을 표시한다.

He is more generous than kind.

(3) 비교급 and 비교급

정도가 점차적으로 높아짐을 표시한다.

The road got worse and worse.

(4) 관용적 표현

- He has not less than(=at least) 5 dollars. '적어도 5불은...'
- She is not less rich than her sister.
  (=She is as rich as, or richer than, her sister.) '나을망정 못하지 않다'
- We expect nothing less than(=only) an attack.
  '오직 공격만이 있으리라는 것쯤은'
- I like her none the less for her faults.(=in spite of)
- He has no more than(=only) 10 dollars. '10불 밖에 없다'
- I am no more mad than you are.
  (=I am not mad anymore than you(are).)
  =You are not mad, nor am I. (너와 마찬가지로 나는 미친 사람이 아니다.)
- He has not more than(=at most) five. '기껏해야 다섯 또는 그 이하'
- A whale is not a fish any more than a horse is.
  (=A whale is no more a fish than a horse is.)
- I have no less than(-as mush as) 10,000 dollars.
  '나는 10,000달러 정도는 지니고 있다'
- She no less than you is beautiful. (그녀는 당신 못지않게 아름답다.)
  cf. Although john is indifferent to alice, she likes him no less for it.
  (= None the less, not the less '그래도, 여전히')
- She is no less rich than (=as rich as) her sister. '못지않게'

3. 최상급의 기본 용법

① John is the happiest in his class.

② The richest man in the world can never get it.

③ Nothing is so pretty as this.

= Nothing is prettier than this.

= This is prettier than anything else.

= This is the prettiest of all.

(1) 셋 이상의 것 중에서 정도가 최대인 것을 표시한다.

The coldest month of the year is January.

(2) 최상급은 때로는 'even'의 뜻을 내포하는 수가 있다.

The greatest(=even the greatest) scholar does not know everything.

(3) 원급 또는 비교급을 사용하여서도 최상급과 동등한 뜻을 표시할 수 있다.

No other boy in the class is so tall as Jim.

= No other boy in the class is taller than Jim.

= Jim is taller than any other boy in this class.

= Jim is the tallest boy in this class.

II. Sentence Structure

1. The man was always _____ to old people.
   (A) respectable (B) respective
   (C) respectful (D) respecting

2. _____ students were playing in the playground.
   (A) Hundred of (B) Hundreds of
   (C) Two hundreds (D) Two hundreds of

3. _____ ended in 1945.
   (A) World War two (B) World War second
   (C) Two World War (D) Second World War

4. I prefer coffee _____ tea at breakfast.
   (A) to (B) than
   (C) or (D) and

5. He is older than I _____ two years.
   (A) as (B) so
   (C) or (D) by

6. He is a very _____ person.
   (A) society (B) sociable
   (C) sociably (D) socially

7. He made his _____ speech at Keimyung University.
   (A) historical (B) historic
   (C) history (D) historian

연구 및 정답

1. (C) respectable 존경할만한, respective 각각의, respectful 공손한.
2. (B) Two hundred 200 명, Hundreds of 수백의.
3. (A) World War II(Two); The second World War.
4. (A) prefer A to B: B보다 A를 더 좋아하다.
5. (D) by 정도의 전치사.
6. (B) sociable 사교적인.
7. (B) historical 역사적, 역사학의 historic 역사에 남을만한, 역사적인.

1. This area is a very _____ source of oil and minerals.
   (A) real (B) right
   (C) ripe (D) rich

2. He spent a _____ amount of money on the purchase of the house.
   (A) consideration (B) considerate
   (C) considerable (D) considering

3. The information in this brochure is _____ to everyone before next month.
   (A) understandable (B) efficient
   (C) informed (D) available

4. To our surprise, he is going to take _____ retirement.
   (A) sooner (B) early
   (C) ready (D) previous

5. All of the board members will be invited to a _____ dinner party.
   (A) form (B) previous
   (C) former (D) formal

6. A major _____ goal of this year is to improve the quality of each product.
   (A) strategies (B) strategize
   (C) strategic (D) strategy

7. Some batteries are short-lived, so it is recommended that you buy_____ batteries.
   (A) rechargeable (B) recharger
   (C) recharged (D) recharging

연구 및 정답

1. (D) rich 부유한, 풍부한, 비옥한.
2. (C) considerable 상당한, considerate 사려깊은.
3. (D) available 유효한, 이용 가능한.
4. (B) early retirement 조기 퇴직.
5. (D) former 전의, formal 정식적인.
6. (C) 형용사 + 명사 구조.
7. (A) 형용사 + 명사 구조.

1. The decision of the government was _____.
   (A) shocked (B) shocking
   (C) shock (D) the shock of

2 More and more people became _____ about our environment.
   (A) concerned (B) concerning
   (C) concern (D) the concern of

3. *The Animal Farm*, written by George O'Well, is popular and _____ today.
   (A) appealed (B) appealing
   (C) appeal (D) the appeal

4. _____ he say that again.
   (A) Never will (B) Never do
   (C) Never is (D) Never have

5. Our test results were _____ because we all did _____ on the test.
   (A) good - good (B) good - well
   (C) well - good (D) well - well

6. This computer has more functions and it is _____ that one.
   (A) twice expensiver than (B) more twice expensive than
   (C) as twice expensive as (D) two times as expensive as

7. This is _____ the world.
   (A) most beautiful city of (B) the beautifulest city in
   (C) the most beautiful city of (D) the most beautiful city in

연구 및 정답

1. (B) 결정이 충격을 주는 주체.
2. (A) 사람들이 걱정을 하는 즉 수동의 의미를 지님.
3. (B) appealing 매력을 주는, 매력적인.
4. (A) 부정부사 강조 구조; 도치 현상.
5. (B) 보어로는 형용사, 동사 수식은 부사.
6. (D) 알맞은 배수사 표현?
7. (D) 최상급 표현.

Ⅲ. Grammar Practice

1. Yellowstone is(A) a well(B) place for(C) animals to live in.(D)

2. Ants build(A) their cities(B) in(C) much(D) places.

3. Too(A) many(B) alcohol can(C) make you sick(D).

4. Sharks keep(A) the oceans cleanly(B) because(C) they eat sick fish(D) and animals.

5. Cereal(A) is a(B) very commonly(C) breakfast in(D) the United States.

6. There(A) are(B) much(C) different kinds of(D) dances.

7. People love(A) jeans because(B) they(C) are comfortably(D).

연구 및 정답

1. (B) good place으로 바꿔야 한다. well 은 건강한, 잘.
2. (D) many + 복수 가산명사, much + 불가산 명사.
3. (B) many + 복수 가산명사, much + 불가산 명사.
4. (B) 보어로는 형용사가 옴.
5. (C) 형용사 + 명사.
6. (C) many + 복수 가산명사, much + 불가산 명사.
7. (D) 보어로는 형용사가 옴.

1. Expected (A) noises are usually (B) more tolerable (C) than unexpected ones of the alike (D) magnitude.

2. Humans utilize (A) their front (B) teeth for biting (C) and their behind (D) teeth for chewing.

3. Good puzzles (A) provide an excellent (B) way to explore the realm of thought abstract (C) best known to mathematicians (D).

4. During (A) dreams the body is asleep but (B) the thinking part (C) of the brain is awake wide (D).

5. Some (A) antibiotics used in (B) the treatment of human disease are like (C) only in that they are obtained (D) from fungi and bacteria.

6. The more (A) uncomfortably (B) he felt, the less (C) he participated (D).

7. Rabbits and hares look (A) much like (B) and are often mistaken for (C) each other (D).

연구 및 정답

1. (D) 형용사 alike는 서술적으로만 사용된다. alike → same.
2. (D) behind → back.
3. (C) 형용사 abstract가 명사 thought앞에 놓여야 한다.
4. (D) 부사 wide는 형용사 awake 앞에 놓여야 함.
5. (C) 서술적 용법 alike.
6. (B) 주격보어로는 형용사가 옴.
7. (B) 서술적 용법 alike.

Ⅳ. Vocabulary

※ Choose the one which has the closest meaning with the underlined part.

1. He was so <u>bewildered</u> that he didn't know what to do.
   (A) amused (B) enjoyed
   (C) perplexed (D) excited

2. Many kinds of animals are now <u>no longer existing</u>.
   (A) partial (B) neutral
   (C) amiss (D) extinct

3. How long does the contract <u>hold good</u>?
   (A) feel for (B) remain valid
   (C) requir (D) call for

4. Jimmy was born in Pennsylvania but <u>brought up</u> in California.
   (A) adopted (B) kidnapped
   (C) died (D) educated and trained

5. Many people <u>were bound for</u> the trade fair.
   (A) were going to (B) were obliged to
   (C) were busy with (D) were returning to

6. They <u>turned down</u> my application for the job because I didn't know German.
   (A) accept (B) postpone
   (C) reject (D) reconsider

7. The construction of a bridge <u>calls for</u> a lot of money.
   (A) requires (B) supplies
   (C) provides (D) visits

연구

1. bewilder 난처하게 만들다, 당황하게 하다(=puzzle, perplex).
2. extinct 꺼진, 다한, 전멸한, 멸종한.
3. hold good 효력이 있다, 유효하다 (=remain valid, be effective).
4. bring up 교육하다, 양육하다(=educate, rear).
5. be bound for 으로 향하다.
6. turn down 거절하다.
7. call for 요구하다.

정답

1. C 2. D 3. B 4. D 5. A 6. C 7. A

1. Evolution has hardly changed the horse-shoe crab over millions of years.
   (A) carefully (B) probably
   (C) scarcely (D) slowly

2. The fragrant scent of the lilac is said to herald the beginning of spring.
   (A) symbolize (B) hasten
   (C) exult (D) announce

3. San Francisco's Chinese community, comprising 67,000 inhabitants, is the largest concentration of Chinese outside of Asia.
   (A) adults (B) workers
   (C) visitors (D) residents

4. Bob, who has come late to every meeting we have held, surprised us today by being punctual.
   (A) on time (B) in time
   (C) at no time (D) in no time

5. They already presented a wide ethnic diversity.
   (A) instrumental (B) artistic
   (C) ethical (D) racial

6. Such activities would be favorable to interest.
   (A) lucid (B) deductive
   (C) delusive (D) advantageous

7. He can not accede to the terms.
   (A) yield to (B) listen to
   (C) agree to (D) argue to

연구

1. hardly: barely, scarcely, narrowly, nearly.
2. herald: announce, bring news, proclaim, shout.
3. inhabit: reside, lodge, dwell, stay.
4. punctual: on time.
5. ethenic: racial.
6. favorable: advantageous.
7. accede to: agree to.

정답

1. C 2. D 3. D 4. A 5. D 6. D 7. C

CHAPTER 6

ADVERB

I. Grammar Focus

A. 부사의 기능

동사, 형용사, 부사, 대명사, 문장을 수식하는 기능을 한다.

· He did it easily. (동사수식)

· The room is big **enough** for five people. (형용사 수식)

· He studied English **very** well. (부사수식)

· Only Tom knows the answer. (명사 수식)

· Happily, he did not die. (문장수식)

B. 부사의 형태

(1) beautiful-beautifully, happy-happily, true-truly, probable-probably.

(2) He was late for class. (형용사)

He came home **late** last light. (부사: 늦게)

I haven't seen him **lately**. (부사: 최근에)

(3) 형용사와 동형인 경우와 -ly가 붙는 경우

We went **direct** to the station. (=straight)

He left **directly** after breakfast. (=at once)

I saw up **late** night. (늦도록)

I haven't seen him **lately**. (요즘)

Draw **near** and listen. (가까이)

I was **nearly** killed. (~할 뻔하다)

Key Point 1

downstair, upstair를 부사로 만들 때는 downstairs upstairs로

He ran downstairs to get the book.
She went upstairs to go to bed.

Key Point 2

명사+ly는 부사가 아니라 형용사가 된다.

love → lovely(사랑스러운)
friend → friendly(친근한)
home → homely(가정의)
man → manly(사내다운)
woman → womanly(여성다운)
time → timely(적절한)
father → fatherly(부정의)

He has had a friendly relation with her.
It is manly for him to do such a thing.

C. 부사의 위치

- The sun always rises in the east.
  She is always cheerful.
- Put on your hat.
  Put your hat on.
  Put it in.
- We arrived here safely yesterday.
- safely at the station.

(1) 빈도, 정도부사의 위치 :

일반 동사의 앞, Be, 조동사의 뒤에 위치한다.

→ always, often, sometimes, scarcely, hardly, seldom, ever, never...

He is always late for school.

We usually eat supper at six.

(2) 타동사+부사의 결합 :

"타동사 부사 목적어", "타동사 목적어 부사"가 모두가능.

하나 목적어가 대명사일 경우 '타동사 목적어 부사' 만 가능하다

He took his hat off. (O)

He took off his hat. (O)

He put it on. (O)

He put on it. (X)

(3) 2개 이상의 부사(구)사용 :

문미에 위치하여 "장소 + 방법·빈도 + 시간" 의 순서로 결정한다.

John went <u>to the library</u> <u>every night</u> <u>during December</u>.
장소 빈도 시간

He arrived <u>here</u> <u>safely</u> <u>last light</u>.
장소 방법 시간

I immediately went <u>to the hospital</u> <u>by car</u> <u>last night</u>.
장소 방법 시간

(4) 동일 성격이 올 경우 :

"작은 단위 + 큰 단위"의 순서로 정리

I met him <u>at his house</u> <u>in Seoul</u>.
(좁은 장소) (넓은 장소)

He was born <u>at a small village</u> <u>in New york</u> <u>on August 2nd</u>, <u>1917</u>.
(좁은 장소) (넓은 장소) (짧은 시간) (긴 시간)

Key Point 3

"still"의 위치는 빈도부사의 위치와 동일하며, "부정의 조동사" 앞에 위치한다.

He is **still** in bed.
She **still** dislikes him.
She **still** doesn't speak English well.
I **still** can't believe what he said.

Key Point 4

문두부사, 문장수식, 문장에 대한 부연설명을 할 경우 부사는 문두에 위치한다.

Certainly, he is behaving well. → It is certain that he is behaving well.
Wisely, John returned the money. → John was wise to return the money.
Happily, he was not hurt. → I am happy that he was not hurt.
Frankly speaking, he is not up to the job. → If I speak frankly, he is not up to the job.

D. 주의할 부사의 용법

1. very-much

① A **very** large building, **very** much, **very** amusing (형용사, 부사, 현재 분사를 수식)

I don't sing **very** well. (그다지 ~이 아니다.)

② He is **much** better today. (비교급, 최상급 수식)

This is **much** the best.

③ It doesn't matter very **much**. (동사수식)

④ I am much misunderstood. (과거분사수식)

cf. A **very** tired look on his face.

I am **very** concerned about his health.

He was **very** pleased. (delighted, surprised, worried, frightened, interested, tired, troubled, excited, worn.)

⑤ I am very **much** afraid. (서술형용사나 형용사구 수식)

He was **much** at a loss.

※ very는 형용사, 부사, 현재분사를 수식하며, much는 동사, 과거분사, 서술형용사 (a~), 비교급, 최상급, 부사구 등을 수식한다.

2. already – yet 와 still – anymore

① I have **already** been to America three times.

I haven't visited Berlin **yet**.

② Have you finished your homework **yet**?

cf. Has the plane **already** left the airport?

③ He is **still** hoping for a letter from her.

Mary doesn't play the piano **any more**.

※ still은 긍정문에서 「아직 ~ 하고 있다」의 의미이며 any more는 부정문에서 「이제는~아니다」, already는 긍정문에서 「이미, 벌써」 yet는 부정, 의문문에서 「아직 벌써」의 뜻.

3. yes-no

① Isn't it beautiful?	Yes, it is. (예, 그렇습니다.)
Are you coming or not?	Yes, I am coming. (예, 가겠습니다.)
② Won't you come?	No, I won't. (예, 안 가겠습니다.)
Does he breathe?	No, he is dead. (아니오, 그는 죽었습니다.)

※ yes는 앞 문장의 내용을 긍정적으로 받을 때, no는 부정적으로 받을 때 사용된다.

4. ago-before-since

① He came up to Seoul ten years **ago**. (지금부터 ~ 전에)

② Ha had come up to Seoul ten years **before**. (그때부터 ~ 전에)

I haven't seen him **before**. (전에)

③ I met him five years ago, but have not seen him **since**. (그 후 지금까지)

5. rather-fairly

① He is **fairly** clever, but she is **rather** stupid. (그는 정말 똑똑하지만, 그녀는 꽤 바보같다.)

② That girl is **rather** pretty. (퍽, rather가 좋은 뜻에 쓰일 때)

③ I want something **rather** smaller than this. (「좀」, 비교급에는 rather)

6. ever의 뜻

① Have you ever seen a bear? (의문, 조건문에서 - 언젠가)

② Nothing ever happened in this village. (부정, 최상급에서 - 지금까지)

This picture is the most beautiful I have **ever** seen.

cf. It is more necessary than **ever**. (어느 때보다)

③ Who **ever** told you that? (의문문에-「도대체」 = 「on earth」)

④ That boy is **ever** ready to help. (「언제나 · 항상」 – 주로 관용구에)

Work **as** hard **as** **ever**.

II. Sentence Structure

1. It's _____ cold.
   (A) terror (B) terrify
   (C) terrible (D) terribly

2. They have certainly studied _____ to pass the test.
   (A) hard enough (B) hardly enough
   (C) enough hard (D) enough hardly

3. He made a presentation very _____ at the annual conference.
   (A) hesitate (B) hesitant
   (C) hesitantly (D) hesitation

4. Mr. Lee is a _____ efficient employee in the human resources division.
   (A) high (B) highly
   (C) higher (D) height

5. The doctor _____ recommended the healthy diet to the patient.
   (A) strong (B) strength
   (C) strengthen (D) strongly

6. The profits were reduced _____, compared to last quarter's.
   (A) substantially (B) substantial
   (C) substance (D) substancing

7. _____, our company didn't get the contract for some reason.
   (A) Unfortune (B) Unfortunately
   (C) Unfortunate (D) Misfortune

연구 및 정답

1. (D) 부사 + 형용사.
2. (A) 형용사, 부사 + enough to 부정사 구조.
3. (C) 부사 + 부사.
4. (B) 부사 + 형용사.
5. (D) 동사 수식어구는?
6. (A) 과거분사도 형용사 역할이므로 부사가 수식함.
7. (B) 문장 전체를 수식.

1. I went _____.
   (A) to school everyday slowly
   (B) to school slowly everyday
   (C) slowly everyday to school
   (D) slowly to school everyday

2. Dinner is ready; let's go _____.
   (A) downstairs
   (B) to downstairs
   (C) downstair
   (D) to downstair

3. She _____ experience in her diary.
   (A) usually writes down her
   (B) writes usually down her
   (C) writes down usually her
   (D) usually her writes down

4. The seminar began _____ after the manager left the office.
   (A) briefly
   (B) shortly
   (C) sooner
   (D) rightly

5. The venture company launched the _____ designed product.
   (A) renewal
   (B) never
   (C) newly
   (D) new

6. Prices rise more _____ than wages in times of inflation.
   (A) highly
   (B) easily
   (C) shortly
   (D) quickly

7. Professors are _____ asked to check the attendance rate of students.
   (A) regularly
   (B) regulate
   (C) regular
   (D) regularity

연구 및 정답

1. (B) 〈장소 + 방법 + 시간〉의 어순.
2. (A) downstair는 부사임에 유의.
3. (A) 빈도부사의 위치(be동사/조동사 뒤, 본동사 앞).
4. (B) shortly after 직후.
5. (C) 부사 + 형용사(현분, 과분 포함) + 명사.
6. (D) 뜻으로 파악하는 형용사 용법.
7. (A) 부사 + 형용사(-ing, pp).

1. He was very busy and _____ ever enjoyed free time with his family.
   (A) nearly (B) near
   (C) hardly (D) just

2. He has been meeting with them since the 15th of May, but he _____ hasn't signed an agreement.
   (A) further (B) still
   (C) already (D) yet

3. According to a recent study, only a quarter of managers' time is spent _____.
   (A) productively (B) productive
   (C) productivity (D) productiveness

4. This new way of communication is _____ popular with the younger generation.
   (A) increase (B) increasing
   (C) increased (D) increasingly

5. There have been a lot of complaints about Sarah's performance _____.
   (A) late (B) lately
   (C) latter (D) last

6. Louisa _____ ever misses a work deadline.
   (A) hard (B) hardly
   (C) harden (D) hardness

7. The proposal was so popular, the committee voted _____ to approve it.
   (A) slightly (B) unanimously
   (C) strictly (D) relatively

연구 및 정답

1. (C) 부정부사 hardly가 의미로 맞다.
2. (B) 아직 -않다(still not/ not- yet 구조).
3. (A) 동사 수식어구는?
4. (D) 형용사 + 부사.
5. (B) late 늦은, 늦게, lately 최근에.
6. (B) 부정부사 필요.
7. (B) unanimously 만장일치로.

Ⅲ. Grammar Practice

1. Middle class values are generally normally the dominant values in a society.
(A: Middle class, B: generally normally, C: values, D: a society)

2. Because magnesium is such plentiful in sea water, it is available to most of the countries that want to use it.
(A: Because, B: such, C: available to, D: most of)

3. A chemical element is a substance that cannot be broken down chemical into simpler substances.
(A: substance that, B: be broken, C: chemical, D: simpler)

4. Most talc is used in ceramics and roofing because it resists fire good.
(A: Most, B: used, C: because, D: good)

5. Practical all of the Bering Sea water comes from the Pacific Ocean.
(A: Practical, B: all, C: water, D: from)

6. According to many schools, sociology must necessity be concerned with the problems of justice, especially in matters pertaining to government and economics.
(A: According, B: necessity, C: especially, D: pertaining)

7. The discovery of x-rays in 1895 by W.C. Roentgen was pure accidental.
(A: discovery, B: by W.C. Roentgen, C: was, D: pure)

연구 및 정답

1. (B) generally와 normally는 의미 중복을 초래한다. 어느 하나를 삭제해야 함.
2. (B) 원급 즉 형용사 plentiful을 수식하기 위해서는 very가 적합하다.
3. (C) 동사수식은 부사 chemically가 적합하다.
4. (D) 동사 resists를 수식하기 위해서는 D를 well로 바꾼다.
5. (A) 영어에서 all을 수식할 수 있는 한정사는 없으므로 A를 practically로 바꾼다.
6. (B) necessity → necessarily.
7. (D) accidential은 형용사이므로 그 앞에는 부사형이 옳다.

1. Recent, the elderly man in the wheelchair hired a young man as a companion.
   (A: Recent / B: in the / C: hired / D: companion)

2. Barrett had to lie on his left side all night, and the pain from the wrenched shoulder became some worse.
   (A: had / B: left / C: from / D: some)

3. The sizes to atoms vary regularize throughout the periodic system.
   (A: sizes / B: regularize / C: throughout / D: system)

4. No matter how hard he is working, he will insist on the principle as hardly as he can.
   (A: No matter how / B: insist / C: on / D: hardly)

5. The invitations to the dance indicated that everyone should be dressed formerly.
   (A: The invitations / B: the dance / C: everyone / D: formerly)

6. Influenza travels exactly as fastly as man. In oxcart days its progress was slow.
   (A: travels / B: fastly / C: oxcart days / D: slow)

7. The following night Bill returned quite lately from work to find his wife lying unconscious beside the phone.
   (A: following / B: lately / C: to find / D: lying)

연구 및 정답

1. (A) Recent는 형용사이며 그 다음에 명사가 없으므로 부사형인 Recently로 고쳐야 옳다.
2. (D) 형용사 worse 수식을 위해서는 부사 somewhat이 필요.
3. (B) 동사 수식은 부사 regularize → regularly.
4. (D) as hard as he can.
5. (D) formerly는 former '이전의' 부사이므로 문맥으로 보아 '격식에 맞추어, 정식으로'의 뜻을 가진 formally가 타당함.
6. (B) fast는 형용사, 부사가 같은 형태임.
7. (B) late 늦은, 늦게 lately 최근에.

Ⅳ. Vocabulary

※ Choose the one which has the closest meaning with the underlined part.

1. He had the conviction that everything would happen as he wished.
   (A) great hope (B) mistaken idea
   (C) strong belief (D) personal opinion

2. Thrift is the source of wealth.
   (A) good health (B) finance
   (C) economy (D) property

3. The students handed in their papers this morning.
   (A) distributed (B) bequeathed
   (C) submitted (D) surrendered

4. Mr. Kim is every inch a gentleman.
   (A) every time (B) inch by inch
   (C) completely (D) only

5. The clerk had to break off the conservation in order to wait on a customer.
   (A) start (B) continue
   (C) postpone (D) interrupt

6. The color of most fish matches that of their surroundings.
   (A) ancestors (B) diet
   (C) environment (D) enemies

7. He is assiduous in his studies.
   (A) sincere (B) cordial
   (C) insolent (D) industrious

연구

1. conviction 신념, 설득, 설득당하기, 납득.
2. thrift 검소 절약(economy, frugality).
3. hand in 제출하다(turn in, present, submit).
4. every inch(철두철미) (completely).
5. break off 갑자기 그만두다, 중단하다(interrupt, stop, cut off, hinder).
6. surroundings 환경(environment).
7. assiduous 부지런한(diligent).

정답

1. C 2. C 3. C 4. C 5. D 6. C 7. D

1. A mountain's lower slopes may support grass and timber, although the crest may be barren and snow-covered.
   (A) impressive (B) dangerous
   (C) smooth (D) lifeless

2. A peculiar fact about life on Earth is that the molecules of living things tend to move in a left-ward direction.
   (A) unexpected (B) universal
   (C) unimportant (D) odd

3. In 1928 an expedition to Antartica headed by Richard E. Byrd established the settlement called Little America on the Ross Ice Shelf.
   (A) led (B) equipped
   (C) thought (D) expose

4. The very language, archaic as it may sometimes be, serves to reinforce and broaden the child's vocabulary.
   (A) difficult (B) confused
   (C) remote (D) old

5. The oldest preserved manuscripts are those written on papyrus, which were found in Egyptian tomb.
   (A) protected (B) hidden
   (C) sought (D) discovered

6. Communication is one of the most important bonds that hold cultural systems together.
   (A) obligation (B) qualities
   (C) links (D) needs

7. Structurally, the inside of early Christian churches was simple.
   (A) layout (B) design (C) interior (D) content

연구

1. barren: lifeless.
2. peculiar: odd, queer.
3. head: lead.
4. archaic: old.
5. find: discover.
6. bond: link.
7. inside: interior.

정답

1. D 2. D 3. A 4. D 5. D 6. C 7. C

CHAPTER 7

VOICE

I. Grammar Focus

A. 수동태를 써야 하는 경우

(1) 능동태의 주어가 분명하지 않을 때 :

He **was killed** in the war.

(2) 행위자(능동태의 주어)보다는 동작의 대상(수동태의 주어=능동태의 목적어)에 더 관심이 많을 때 :

Who **was punished** by her?

(3) 앞 문장과의 문맥상 필요가 있을 때 :

He made a speech and **was asked** many question at the end.

(4) 수동태의 의미가 거의 없이 자동사로 느껴지는 경우 :

I **was born** Nov.4, 1958.

(5) 작품, 발명품 등을 나타낼 때 :

Hamlet **was written** by Shakespeare.

(6) 행위자를 나타내지 않으려고 할 때 :

Enough **has been** said of the matter.

B. 주의할 수동태의 용법

1. (능동태) 제4형식 → (수동태)로 전환

4형식 동사 + IO + DO

make, write, send, read, sell, sing…D. O(사물)만이 수동의 주어

forgive, pardon, envy, save…I. O(사람)만이 수동의 주어

He sold me a book. → A book was sold to me by him.

They sent us many presents. → Many presents were sent (to) us.

He forgave me my negligence. → I was forgiven my negligence by him.

She envied him his luck. → He was envied his luck by her.

2. (능동태) 제5형식→(수동태)로 전환

[지각동사, 사역동사] + O + 동사원형

be p.p ~ to부정사로 전환

We saw him enter the room. → He was seen to enter the room.

She let me go there. → I was allowed to go there by her.

3. (능동태) 명령문→(수동태)로 전환

(직접명령) Root+O~ → Let+O+be p.p

(직접명령 : 부정) Don't Root+O → Don't let+O+be+p.p~

Let+O+not+be p.p~

4. (능동태) 의문문→(수동태)로 전환

(1) Who가 주어진 경우 (By whom+be동사+주어+p.p?)

Who saw the accident? [의문문]

Who saw the accident. [평서문 어순 배치]

The accident was seen by whom. [수동태 어순 배치]

By whom was the accident seen? [수동태 의문문]

(2) 기타 의문사가 주어인 경우 (의문사+be동사+주어+p.p?)

What did he write on the blackboard? [능동 의문문]

He wrote what on the blackboard. [평서문 어순 배치]

What was written on the blackboard by him. [수동태의 어순 배치]

What was written on the blackboard by him? [수동 의문문]

5. (능동태)부정주어→(수동태)로 전환 : by+부정행위자는 수동에서 쓰지 못함.

(능동태 주어) ………………………… [수동태]

Nobody ……………………………………not~ by anybody

Nothing ……………………………………not~ by anything

No one ……………………………………not~ by anyone

Nobody could solve the problem.

→ The problem could not be solved(by anybody).

Nothing makes him laugh.

→ He is not made to laugh by anything.

Key Point 1

Any ~ not의 구문은 사용불가

Anyone can't solve the situation perfectly. (X)
No one can solve the situation perfectly. (O)

6. (능동태) 목적어가 명사절→(수동태) 로 전환 : 가주어 It를 사용하는 경우와 that절 속의 주어를 수동태의 주어로 하는 두 가지 경우가 있다.

They say that astronauts are modern heroes.

→ It is said that astronauts are modern heroes.

→ Astronauts are said to be modern heroes.

People say that she has worked hard.

→ It is said that she has worked hard.

→ She is said to have worked hard.

7. (능동태)동사가 타동사구→(수동태)로 전환

타동사구로는

자동사+전치사(laugh at, look at, run over…)

자동사+부사+전치사(speak ill of, look up to, do away with…)

타동사+부사(give up, carry out, put off…)

타동사+목적어+전치사(take care of, pay attention to,…)

는 반드시 묶어서 1개의 동사로 취급한다.

They **laughed** at her.

→ She **was laughed at** by them.

We should **do away with** a bad custom.

→ A bad custom should **be done away with** by us.

Key Point 2

명사 앞에 형용사(good, no, much, little)가 있을 때는 명사를 주어로 한 수동태 가능

The doctor **took good care of** the patient.
→ The patient **was taken good care of** by the doctor.
→ **Good care** was taken of the patient by the doctor.

We **pay little attention to** this matter.
→ This matter **is paid little attention to** by us.
→ **Little attention** is paid to this matter by us.

8. 관용적인 수동태 구문

(1) 신체의 변화, 손상의 의미표현

be born	태어나다.
be wounded	부상을 입다.
be taken ill	병들다.
be situated	위치해 있다.
be seated	앉다.
be possessed of	지니고 있다.

be drowned	익사하다.
be burnt to death	타죽다.
be frozen to death	얼어죽다.
be starved to death	굶어죽다.
be tired with	지치다.
be exhausted with	지쳐버리다.
be held	열리다.
be dressed in	입고 있다.

Many children **were drowned** on the year.

He **was born** in 1975.

(2) 위치, 열중, 종사의 의미표현

occupy oneself in 「~에 종사하다」→ be occupied in

The church is situated on a hill.

(3) 능동수동태(Active-Passive)「능동형으로 수동의 뜻」을 나타내는 경우를 말한다.

① 특수동사 (sell, open, cut, write, read…)

This novel **sells** well. (=is sold)

The door **opened** of itself.

This play **reads** better than it **acts**. (=is read, is acted)

② 수동의 의미 to 부정사

She is **to blame**. (She should be blamed.)

There is no house **to let** about here. (=to be let)

③ 수동의 의미의 진행형

The house is **building**.

The book is **printing now**.

The meal is **cooking**.

be satisfied with	~에 만족하다	be surprised at	~을 보고 놀라다
be gratified with		be astonished at	
be contented with		be startled at	

be separated from	~와 분리하다	be convinced of	~을 확신하다
be composed of	~으로 구성되다	be persuaded of	

Key Point 3

be known+전치사의 의미
be made+전치사

He is known to all the people in this village. 「~에게 알려지다」
The tree is known by its fruit. 「~으로 판단되다」
The city is known for its tall buildings. 「~으로 유명해지다」
He is known as a successful architect. 「~로서 알려지다」
The table is made of wood. (변화방향← : 물리적 변화)
The butter is made from milk. (변화방향← : 화학적 변화)
Grapes are made into wine. (변화방향 : → 결과)

II. Sentence Structure

1. I cannot help _____ my lot.
   (A) being satisfied with
   (B) being satisfied by
   (C) be satisfied with
   (D) satisfy with

2. He doesn't mind _____ by his fellows.
   (A) laugh at
   (B) laughing at
   (C) be laughed at
   (D) being laughed at

3. My sister _____ an American.
   (A) married to
   (B) married with
   (C) was married to
   (D) was married with

4. The mistake has already been _____ by him.
   (A) correct
   (B) correcting
   (C) correction
   (D) corrected

5. The family has _____ from their vacation already.
   (A) return
   (B) returned
   (C) been return
   (D) been returned

6. The conference will _____ in room 448 from 9:00 to 11:00.
   (A) be held
   (B) have held
   (C) hold
   (D) be holding

7. The flight _____ due to heavy snow.
   (A) will cancel
   (B) to be canceled
   (C) cancels
   (D) was canceled

연구 및 정답

1. (A) cannot help~ing ~하지 않을 수 없다, be satisfied with~~에 만족해하다.
2. (D) mind는 동명사를 목적어로 취함.
3. (C) marry(=be married to) ~와 결혼하다.
4. (D) be corrected by 누구에 의해서 바로 잡히다.
5. (B) 가족이 돌아오는 주체가 되므로 능동 구문.
6. (A) 개최되다의 적절한 표현은?
7. (D) 취소되므로 수동 구문.

1. We were surprised _____ the bad news.
   (A) with (B) in
   (C) for (D) at

2. Samsung Co. _____ the building last year.
   (A) was constructed (B) constructed
   (C) has constructed (D) constructs

3. The key to the room should be _____ by noon.
   (A) returning (B) to return
   (C) returned (D) return

4. The bank is _____ near the office building where you work.
   (A) locate (B) locating
   (C) located (D) location

5. Interviews will _____ all afternoon and then will be a small reception.
   (A) conduct (B) are conducting
   (C) have conducted (D) be conducted

6. Companies will be _____ to receive a lot of grants from the government.
   (A) detailed (B) pleased
   (C) responsible (D) previous

7. Employees who want to be _____ for travel expenses need to submit those receipts.
   (A) spent (B) informed
   (C) reimbursed (D) requested

연구 및 정답

1. (D) be surprised at.
2. (B) 과거시제이면서 능동 구문.
3. (C) key가 돌아와야 하므로 수동 구문.
4. (C) be located ~에 위치해 있다.
5. (D) 인터뷰가 이루어지므로 수동 구문.
6. (B) 기뻐하다의 알맞은 표현은?
7. (C) 환급받다의 적절한 표현은?

1. All the lights in the building are _____ by the maintenance team once a month.
   (A) check (B) checking
   (C) checked (D) checks
2. This picture was _____ by a famous photographer.
   (A) take (B) taking
   (C) taken (D) took
3. All payments can _____ by credit card if the amount is over $100.
   (A) make (B) makes
   (C) be making (D) be made
4. The residents _____ 30 days to move out of the building.
   (A) were given (B) gave
   (C) give (D) giving
5. The report _____ by a special committee.
   (A) writes (B) was written
   (C) write (D) are written
6. The director _____ to say that she plans to retire soon.
   (A) hears (B) heard
   (C) was heard (D) was hearing
7. I _____ to do my homework by my parents.
   (A) make (B) makes
   (C) was made (D) were made

연구 및 정답

1. (C) 점검되다.
2. (C) 사진 찍히는 객체의 적절한 표현.
3. (D) 모든 지불을 카드로 할 수 있다의 적절한 표현은?
4. (A) 시간이 주어지다.
5. (B) 보고서가 쓰여 지다.
6. (C) 소식이 들리다.
7. (C) 부모가 주체임.

Ⅲ. Grammar Practice

1. The enemy will, after all, be defeat in a week or so.
   (A: enemy, B: after all, C: defeat, D: or so)

2. It is say that many accidents are caused by careless driving.
   (A: say, B: many, C: caused, D: careless driving)

3. Louisa May Alcott is chiefly remembered for *Little Women*, one of the most popular girl's books ever wrote.
   (A: remembered, B: one, C: popular, D: wrote)

4. Despite the evidence of the existence of small amounts of water vapor and ice crystals on Mars, its atmosphere is know to be extremely dry.
   (A: Despite, B: small amounts, C: is know, D: extremely)

5. The constitution provides that no president can be elect more than twice.
   (A: provides, B: no, C: be elect, D: more than)

6. The Hall of Fame was found with the help of a gift from Helen Miller Gould.
   (A: The Hall of Fame, B: found, C: the help, D: from)

7. This phenomenon has describe so often as to need no further cliches on the subject here.
   (A: phenomenon, B: has describe, C: further, D: on)

연구 및 정답

1. (C) 격퇴당하다.
2. (A) 말해진다는 표현은?
3. (D) books (which(that) were) ever written.
4. (C) be known to.
5. (C) be+pp의 형태 필요.
6. (B) find-found-found 찾다, found-founded-founded 설립하다, a gift from 사람 ~로부터의 선물, 기부금.
7. (B) 대상을 나타내므로 has been described.

1. The <u>first</u> (A) short story <u>publish</u> (B) by Washing Irving <u>was</u> (C) *Rip Van Winkle*, <u>which</u> (D) appeared in 1819.

2. It is <u>not easy</u> (A) to write <u>good history</u> (B) even if <u>all the</u> (C) facts could be known and <u>documents</u> (D).

3. Cottage cheese, <u>an American favorite</u> (A), <u>can made</u> (B) easily <u>at home</u> (C) <u>from</u> (D) milk, lemon juice, and salt.

4. <u>They are believed</u> (A) that people <u>should</u> (B) learn to dive <u>when</u> (C) they <u>are learning</u> (D) to swim.

5. <u>An old</u> (A) city, Saint Augustine, Florida, <u>was founded</u> (B) in 1565 <u>by the</u> (C) Spanish <u>explorer</u> (D), Pedro Menedez de Aviles.

6. It <u>is saying</u> (A) that <u>a buried</u> (B) treasure <u>was hidden</u> (C) <u>near here</u> (D).

7. <u>Bacteria</u> (A) and viruses are <u>too small</u> (B) <u>to see</u> (C) by the <u>naked eyes</u> (D).

연구 및 정답

1. (B) story를 수식하는 분사가 필요 published.
2. (D) 등위 접속사로 연결된 부분은 평형구조 documented.
3. (B) can be made.
4. (A) They believe; It is believed.
5. (B) 발견되다와 설립하다의 차이점은?
6. (A) It is said that S + V ~.
7. (C) to be seen.

Ⅳ. Vocabulary

※ Choose the one which has the closest meaning with the underlined part.

1. Young people are vulnerable to the influences of radio and television.
   (A) persuaded by (B) appeased by
   (C) programed (D) susceptible to

2. Many of his colleagues eventually agreed that Einstein's theory was tenable.
   (A) tenuous (B) warrantable
   (C) redundant (D) tolerate

3. The introduction of standardized parts was a great contribution to the automobile industry.
   (A) neutralized (B) spare
   (C) uniform (D) production

4. A major characteristic of parliamentary government is the fusion of executive and legislative powers in one body.
   (A) union (B) fixing
   (C) strength (D) alignment

5. Millennia have passed since the pyramids were built.
   (A) Hundreds of years (B) Millions of decades
   (C) Several centuries (D) Thousands of years

6. In 1939 the stock market began its catastrophic plunge.
   (A) disastrous (B) unequaled
   (C) unforseen (D) deliberate

7. Maria has a provisional license.
   (A) permanent (B) regional
   (C) temporary (D) illegal

연구

1. vulnerable 영향을 받기 쉬운. appeased by ~에 진정해 하는.
2. tenable 믿을 만한. tenuous 보잘것없는. 빈약한. redundant 여분의.
3. standardized 표준화 된.
4. fusion 융합, 제휴(alignment).
5. millennia: millennium(천년)의 복수형.
6. disastrous 파국적인, 재앙의. unforeseen 예상할 수 없는. deliberate 숙고하는, 숙고하다.
7. provisional 임시의. permanent 영구적인. illegal 불법적인.

정답

1. D 2. B 3. C 4. A 5. D 6. A 7. C

1. By what criterion will you judge the theory?
   (A) consideration (B) standard
   (C) result (D) decision

2. Helen and Bob were childless, yet all tests showed that they were not sterile.
   (A) infertile (B) contemptuous
   (C) resonable (D) futile

3. I don't think it is impartial of the teacher to flunk my biology exam.
   (A) unbiased (B) effusive
   (C) compatible (D) exonerative

4. The weary motorist finally found a motel.
   (A) wounded (B) credible
   (C) tired (D) cautious

5. His evidence refuted the charges.
   (A) confirmed (B) analyzed
   (C) cleared (D) disproved

6. He was a prolific writer.
   (A) esteemed (B) famous
   (C) productive (D) celebrated

7. The discontinued students retaliated by boycotting the school cafeteria.
   (A) vindicated (B) took revenge
   (C) retrieved (D) retracted

연구

1. criterion 기준. consideration 사고, 고려. standard 기준.
2. sterile 불모의, 불임의. futile 효과가 없는, 쓸데없는. contemptuous 경멸하는.
3. impartial 공정한(= unbiased). effusive 심정을 토로하는. exonerative 면죄의.
4. weary 피곤한.
5. refute disprove (반박하다). confirm 확인하다.
6. prolific 다산의, 많이 생기는. esteem 존경하다.
7. retaliate 응수하다, 보복하다. vindicate 혐의를 풀다. retrieve 보상하다. retract 물러서게 하다, 철회하다.

정답

1. B 2. A 3. A 4. C 5. D 6. C 7. B

CHAPTER 8

INFINITIVE

I. Grammar Focus

A. 부정사의 시제

He seems **to be** idle.

He seems **to have been** idle.

(1) 단순부정사(to Root) : 문장의 시제 동일 또는 하나 나중시제 표시

(2) 완료부정사(to have pp) : 시제가 다르다

He seems **to be** diligent.	He seems **to have been** diligent.
(=It seems that he is diligent.	(=It seems that he **was** diligent.)
He seemed **to be** diligent.	He seemed **to have been** diligent.
(=It seemed that he was diligent.)	(=It seemed that he **had been** diligent.)

Key Point 1

hope, wish, expect, intend, promise, forget+to Root는 미래를 나타낸다.

I hope to see you soon.
(=I hope that I shall see you soon.)
He hoped to write to me.
(=He hoped that he would write to me.)

B. 명사적 용법

- It is difficult **to speak** a foreign language.
- All she does is **to complain**.
- I think it better **to start** at once.
- He knows better than **to do** such a thing.
- Please tell me **which magazine to buy**.

① 주어로 사용 (가주어 · 진주어 용법)

To see you is always a pleasure. → **It** is always a pleasure **to see** you.

② 보어로 사용 : Tom's hobby is **to collect** stamps.

③ 목적어로 사용 (가목적어 · 진목적어 용법)

I found **it** difficult **to explain** his behavior.

I make **it** a rule **to take** a walk.

Key Point 2

"but, except, than, save, about(전치사)"는 부정사를 목적어로 취함

I have nothing to do except do it.
She is about to go to the movies.
He has no choice but to laugh.

Key Point 3

"의문사 + to Root~"는 "~인지를"의 의미로 사용

I don't know how to drive a car. (=how I should drive a car.)
I don't make up my mind where to go. (=where I should go.)
She will tell you what to do. (=what she should do.)

C. 형용사적 용법

- You will find something **to interest** you there.
- The time at which **to arrive** is 8 p.m.
- She is **to get married** next spring.

① 명사· 대명사를 수식하는 경우

② "전치사 + 관계대명사 + to Root"가 명사를 수식하는 경우

③ "Be-to"용법

You **are to finish** the work by noon. (의무)

He **is to meet** her at six o'clock. (예정)

Not a soul **is to be seen** on the street. (가능)

If you **are to succeed**, you must work hard. (의지)

He **was never to see** his wife and children. (운명)

Key Point 4

전치사의 목적격 관계

I can't find anything **to sit on**.
She has no income **to live on**.
This apron has no pocket **to put** things **into**.
He has a pen **to write with**.

D. 부사적 용법

- He went to England **to study** English literature. (목적)
- She grew up **to be** a poetess. (결과)
- I am very happy **to see** you again. (원인)
- He must be crazy **to treat** you like this. (이유·판단)
- **To hear** her sing, you might take her for a singer. (조건)
- The girl is pleasant **to talk with**. (형용사 수식)

Key Point 5

목적 · 결과의 관용구

I worked hard **in order to** pass the test.
→ I worked hard **so as to** pass the test.
→ I worked hard **so that** I could pass the test.

He was **so** tall **as to** touch the ceiling.
→ He was tall **enough to** touch the ceiling.
→ He was **so** tall **that** he **could** touch the ceiling.

The box is **too** heavy for me to carry.
→ The box is **so** heavy **that** I **can't** carry it.

E. 독립 부정사, 원형부정사, 대부정사

- To do him justice, he is an honest man.
  To start with, he is too young.
- We heard the birds sing cheerfully.
  You had better stay at home.
- A : Would you like to come with me?
  B : I'd love to, but I don't have time.

1. 독립부정사 : 문장전체를 수식하며 관용적으로 사용

so to speak	말하자면	to do ~ justice	~을 공정히 평가한다면
to begin with	우선	to be frank with you	솔직히 말한다면
to be sure	확실히	to tell the truth	사실을 말하자면
to make matter worse	설상가상으로	needless to say	말할 필요도 없이

not to speak of~ 「~은 말할 것도 없이」
(=not to mention~, to say nothing of~, let alone~)

2. 원형부정사

- had better+원형「~하는 게 더 낫다(=may(might) as well+원형」

  You **had better start** at once.

- cannot(choose) but + 원형「~하지 않을 수 없다(=cannot help~ing)」

  I **cannot but admire** his courage.

- do nothing but+원형「~하기만 하다」

  They **do nothing but complain.**

- would rather+원형「차라리~하겠다」

  I **would rather not accept** the offer.

- would rather+원형~than+원형「…하느니 차라리~하겠다」

  I **would rather die than surrender.**

- may(might) as well+원형「~하는 게 더 낫다(=had better+원형)」

  You **may as well** apologize to him.

- may well+원형「~하는 것도 당연하다(=have good(very) reason to 부정사)」

  You **may well say** so.

- would(had) sooner+원형~(than+원형…)

  = would(had) as soon+원형~(as+원형…)「(…하느니)차라리 ~하겠다」

  = would(had) rather+원형~(than+원형…)

  I **would sooner stay** at home **than go** for a walk.

  I **would as soon die as live** in slavery.

3. 대부정사 : 동사의 반복을 피하고 "to"만 사용

You may read this book if you want **to (read).**

He didn't pass the test, but he still hopes **to (pass).**

F. 부정사의 부정·분리부정사

- To be or **not to be**; that is a question.
  The teacher told me **never to be** late again.
- I was told **to slowly get up** from the bed.

(1) 부정사의 부정 :

not(never)+(to) 동사 원형

He made haste **in order not to** miss the train.

He tried **not to smile.**

(2) 분리부정사 :

to와 원형사이에 부사를 두어 부정사를 수식하는 것을 분명히 표시

(to+부사+동사의 원형) (단, 주로 구어체에서 많이 사용한다)

To clearly understand it was impossible.

I have tried **to consciously stop** writing about it.

G. 부정사의 의미상 주어

- I hope to pass the test.
- I expect everyone to do his duty.
- It is impossible **for you** to do so.
- It is very kind **of you** to say so.

(1) 의미상 주어=문장의 주어(생략)

I expect to succeed. (=I expect that I will succeed.)

(2) 의미상 주어=문장의 목적어

I expect **him** to succeed. (=I expect that he will succeed.)

(3) 전치사 for의 목적어가 의미상 주어

It is difficult **for her** to read the book.

Is there any need **for us** to hurry?

(4) "of+목적어"가 의미상 주어 : 사람의 성질 형용사가 부정사 앞에 온 경우

(kind, foolish, wise, stupid…)

It's kind **of you** to say so. (=You are kind to say so.)

It's stupid of him to make a mistake. (=He is stupid to make a mistake.)

II. Sentence Structure

1. He seems _____ rich those days.

(A) to be
(B) being
(C) was
(D) to have been

2. He expects _____ soon.

(A) arrive
(B) arrival
(C) to arrive
(D) arriving

3. All I want is _____ to return safe.

(A) he
(B) him
(C) of him
(D) for him

4. Jun went to Seoul _____ with the president of LG company.

(A) for meeting
(B) for meet
(C) to meet
(D) meeting

5. The new workers are expected _____ early tomorrow morning.

(A) arrive
(B) arriving
(C) arrival
(D) to arrive

6. It is important _____ all these directions completely.

(A) to following
(B) following
(C) to follow
(D) follow

7. Our boss promised _____ at the meeting.

(A) to have appeared
(B) to appear
(C) appearing
(D) being appearing

연구 및 정답

1. (D) It seems that he was rich those days. 단문으로.
2. (C) 기대하다는 미래의 뜻을 지니므로 to부정사를 목적어로 취함.
3. (D) 의미상의 주어.
4. (C) 부정사의 목적.
5. (D) expect도 부정사를 취함.
6. (C) It 가주어 to부정사 진주어 구문.
7. (B) 약속하다도 미래의 뜻.

1. It is wise _____ him to read the book.
   (A) for (B) of
   (C) in (D) to

2. It was difficult _____ him to solve the problem.
   (A) for (B) of
   (C) in (D) to

3. She had the man _____ her suitcase.
   (A) to carry (B) carrying
   (C) carry (D) carried

4. She was seen _____ her mother yesterday.
   (A) help (B) to help
   (C) helped (D) to be helped

5. I am planning _____ my sons out to lunch.
   (A) take (B) to take
   (C) taking (D) taken

6. He does not allow students _____ the building after 12 p.m.
   (A) to have entered (B) entered
   (C) entering (D) to enter

7. It is fortunate for me _____ the president in person.
   (A) meeting (B) to meet
   (C) meet (D) met

연구 및 정답

1. (B) 사람의 성질을 나타내는 형용사가 올 때 의미상의 주어 표현은?
2. (A) 그 외 형용사의 의미상 주어 표현 방법은?
3. (C) 사역동사의 목적보어.
4. (B) 지각동사의 수동태 구문.
5. (B) plan to +동사원형.
6. (D) allow + O + to 동사원형.
7. (B) It + for me + to 동사원형 구문.

1. Why did you choose _____ the order?
   (A) cancel (B) to cancel
   (C) cancelling (D) cancelled

2. The committee chairman decided _____ on each member one by one.
   (A) call (B) to call
   (C) calling (D) called

3. She can help you _____ for the conference.
   (A) register (B) to registering
   (C) registering (D) registered

4. I expected my clients _____ to see me.
   (A) come (B) coming
   (C) to come (D) came

5. A sign at the entrance asked shoppers not _____ pets into the store.
   (A) brings (B) to bring
   (C) bringing (D) bring

6. We are very glad _____ with your company on the upcoming projects.
   (A) work (B) to work
   (C) works (D) working

7. It is necessary for us _____ our job on time.
   (A) do (B) does
   (C) doing (D) to do

연구 및 정답

1. (B) choose to 동사원형.
2. (B) decide to 동사원형.
3. (A) help + O + (to) 동사원형.
4. (C) expect + O + to 동사원형.
5. (B) ask + O + to 동사원형.
6. (B) 형용사 수식의 부사 기능의 to 부정사.
7. (D) It + for 목적어 + to 동사원형.

Ⅲ. Grammar Practice

1. Music is one of the best ways to expressing feelings.
   A B C D

2. In 1775, the colonists decided beginning a new country, the United States.
   A B C D

3. Giraffes have eyes that allow them seeing in all directions without twisting their heads.
   A B C D

4. Civilization resulted from the ability of human beings to control fire, cultivate crops, train
   A B C
   animals and built permanent homes.
   D

5. Doctors often study film records of complex operations in order for improving their own
   A B C D
   knowledge and skill.

6. We watched the children to playing soccer in the playground.
   A B C D

7. They had the plumber repaired the broken pipe last week.
   A B C D

연구 및 정답

1. (D) 표현할 형용사적 용법 to express.
2. (B) decide to 동사원형.
3. (B) allow + O + to 동사원형.
4. (D) to control, (to) cultivate, (to) train and (to) build.
5. (C) in order to 동사원형.
6. (B) 지각동사 + O + 동사원형(-ing).
7. (B) 사역동사 + O + 동사원형.

1. At the airport we can see tourists come and to go all day long.
   A B C D

2. It was rude for that man not to take off his hat in the elevator.
   A B C D

3. He deserves to punish for what he did.
   A B C D

4. He has not had a job for a long time, so he has little money to live.
   A B C D

5. Throughout our lives we meet many people, and that is important to be able to judge
   A B C
   what they are like.
   D

6. Body decoration can be used to make someone to feel and look more attractive to others.
   A B C D

7. I did try a lot, but I found that almost impossible to persuade him to change his mind.
   A B C D

연구 및 정답

1. (C) 지각동사 + O + 동사원형(-ing).
2. (B) 사람의 성질을 나타내는 형용사의 의미상 주어 표현은?
3. (B) 벌을 받는다는 수동의 의미.
4. (D) money to live with.
5. (B) it ~ to 동사원형 구조.
6. (B) 사역동사 + O + 동사원형.
7. (C) S + V + 가목적어(it) + OC + 진목적어 구문.

Ⅳ. Vocabulary

※ Choose the one which has the closest meaning with the underlined part.

1. Dried fruit resists rotting much better than fresh fruit.
   (A) decaying (B) cooking
   (C) chewing (D) freezing

2. Unless checked, insects can multiply very rapidly when conditions are in their favor.
   (A) injured (B) controlled
   (C) marked (D) inspected

3. The long-term threat to the survival of elephants is the loss of their natural habitat.
   (A) ivory (B) environment
   (C) allies (D) instincts

4. While at rest, butterflies hold their wings vertically ever their heads.
   (A) tensely (B) upright
   (C) dizzily (D) fast

5. Bats are extremely shy creatures and avoided humans if at all possible.
   (A) timid (B) clean
   (C) private (D) noisy

6. It has been suggested that people who watch television incessantly may become overly passive.
   (A) seriously (B) skeptically
   (C) constantly (D) arbitrarily

7. The gar is a fish with a long, slender body and scales as hard as flint.
   (A) flat (B) straight
   (C) slim (D) fragile

연구

1. rot: decay. chew: bite. freeze: refrigerate.
2. check: control, restrain. injure: damage, harm, hurt. inspect: investigate, examine.
3. habitat 서식지. allies 동맹국. instinct 본능.
4. vertically 곧추서서, 수직으로. dizzy 현기증이 나는.
5. timid 겁이 많은(= shy).
6. incessantly: constantly. skeptically 회의적으로. arbitrarily 자의적으로.
7. slender: slim. fragile 부서지기 쉬운.

정답

1. A 2. B 3. B 4. B 5. A 6. C 7. C

1. Some fairy tales teach children to be brave and persistent.
   (A) courageous (B) obedient
   (C) loyal (D) honest

2. The motor-driven vehicle facilitates business and gives harmless enjoyment to many.
   (A) makes easy (B) makes difficult
   (C) makes rapid (D) makes busy

3. The Pacific Ocean reaches its greatest breadth near the equator.
   (A) depth (B) tepidness
   (C) width (D) beauty

4. His term of office as President will expire next year.
   (A) terminate (B) speed up
   (C) experience (D) begin

5. The simplest of all worms belong to the flat-worm family.
   (A) are bigger than (B) are contrasted with
   (C) are members of (D) are nourishment for

6. Under a blanket of snow the ground is warmer than it would be if it were exposed to the air.
   (A) void (B) storm
   (C) breeze (D) covering

7. An important part of the national government is the Foreign Service, a branch of the Department of State.
   (A) disciple (B) division
   (C) embassy (D) invasion

연구

1. brave: bold, valiant, gallant.
2. facilitate: make easy.
3. breadth: width, (cf. length, thickness).
4. expire: come to an end(=terminate).
5. flat-worm 편충.
7. branch: spread, divide, expend.

정답

1. A 2. A 3. C 4. A 5. C 6. D 7. B

CHAPTER 9

GERUND

I. Grammar Focus

A. 동명사의 기본용법과 형태

Collecting stamps is my hobby. (주어)

We call such an act **cheating.** (보어)

You must avoid **making** such a mistake. (목적어)

There are rules for **introducing** people. (전치사의 목적어)

동명사의 형태

단순형(동사원형 + ing) : 문장과 동일시제

완료형(having p.p) : 문장보다 하나 앞선 시제

She is confident of **winning** the game.

(=She is confident that she **will win** the game.)

I am sure of his **having been** kind.

(=I am sure that he **was** kind.)

B. 동명사의 의미상 주어

- It is foolish behaving like that.

  He succeeded in solving the problem.

  He punished **the student** for being dishonest.

- She insisted on **John('s)** going there.
  I remember her showing me the way.

(1) 의미상 주어=일반인

의미상 주어=주절의 주어, 목적어 생략

Fishing in the lake is forbidden.

I like **playing** the piano.

(2) 의미상 주어는 소유격으로 표시하나 구어에서는 목적격으로 하기도 한다.

(단, 문두는 반드시 소유격)

I don't like **your** speaking ill of others.

Do you mind **me** smoking? (구어)

Him saying so made me anxious. (X)

C. 동명사와 부정사

- (a) I enjoy reading detective stories.
  (b) He refused to pay the bill.
- You must remember to post the letter.
  I remember being paid five dollars.
- He is used to getting up early in the morning.
  She devoted herself to taking care of the poor.

(1) (a) 동명사만을 목적어로 취하는 동사 :

mind, enjoy, give up, admit, postpone, finish, avoid, suggest, consider, include, discontinue

(b) 부정사만을 목적으로 취하는 동사 :

wish, hope, expect, attempt, decide, plan, agree, refuse

(2) remember(forget, regret)+ to 부정사 : 미래사실

remember(forget, regret)+ 동명사 : 과거사실

- I like **playing** the piano. (피아노 치기를 좋아한다.)
  I like **to play** the piano. (지금 피아노를 치고 싶다.)
- I tried **sending** her flowers. (시험삼아 보내 보았다.)
  I tried **to send** her flowers. (보내려고 애썼다.)
- She needs[wants] **helping** = She needs to be helped.
  She needs[wants] **to help** him. (그를 도울 필요가 있다. [돕고 싶다.])

(3) 전치사의 to로 뒤에~ing(동명사)가 오는 경우.

I **object to** [**am opposed to**] being treated like this.

What do you say to taking a rest?

I am **looking forward** to seeing you.

I **am used** to taking exercise regularly.

He **devoted himself** to studying math.

I **fell** to wondering where to go for my holidays.

He went to America **with a view** to studying English.

D. 동명사의 관용적 표현

(1) 「~하지 않을 수 없다.」

I **cannot help** admiring your speech.

= I **cannot but** admire you speech.

= I **cannot choose but** admire your speech.

= I **have no choice but to** admire your speech.

(2) 「~하는 것은 불가능하다.」

There is no knowing how old she is.

= **It is impossible to** know how old she is.

= **We can't** know how old she is.

(3) 「~해도 소용없다.」

It **is no use** trying to persuade him.

= **There is no use in** trying to persuade him.

= **It is of no use to** try to persuade him.

(4) 「자신이 손수 ~한」

This is the peach tree **of my own** planting.

= This is the peach tree **which I myself** planted.

= This is the peach tree **which was** planted **by myself**.

(5) 「~하는 것을 규칙으로 삼다.」

Our family **make a point of** going to church every Sunday.

= Our family are **in the habit of** going to church every Sunday.

= Our family **make it a rule to** go to church every Sunday.

(6) 「~하면 반드시 ~한다.」

I **never** see this watch **without** thinking of you.

= I **never** see this watch **but** I think of you.

but it reminds me of you.

= **Whenever** I see this watch, **I always** think of you.

(7) 「~하자마자 곧」

On(Upon) hearing this news, I changed my plans.

= As soon as / The instant / The moment / The minute / Immediately after ⎤ I heard this news, I changed my plans.

(8) 「~은 말할 것도 없다.」

It goes without saying that she will help us.

= **It is needless to say that** she will help us.

= **It is a matter of course that** she will help us.

(9) 「~하는 것이 어떻겠습니까?」

What do you say to having a cup of coffee?

= **What do you think about having** a cup of coffee?

= **How about having** a cup of coffee?

= **Let's have** a cup of coffee, **shall we**?

(10) 「…하러 갔다.」

We **went** shopp**ing**. / swimm**ing**. / hik**ing**. / fish**ing**.

(11) 「~을 기대하다.」

She **looks forward to** see**ing** you at the party.

= She **expects to** see you at the party.

(12) 「~하고 싶다.」

I don't **feel like** go**ing** to the movies tonight.

= I don't **feel inclined to** go to the movies tonight.

(13) 「~할 목적으로」

He went to England **with a view to** study**ing**[to study] linguistics.

= He went to England **for the purpose of** study**ing** linguistics.

(14) 「막 … 하려는 찰나에 있었다.」

He was on the [point / verge / brink] of leaving.

(15) 「~할 가치가 있다.」

This novel is worth reading.

= It is worthwhile to read this novel.

(16) 「~는 버릇이 있다, ~이 습관 되어 있다.」

He is accustomed to rising at dawn.

= He is used to rising at dawn.

= He is in the habit of rising at dawn.

(17) 「거의~할 뻔하다.」

He [came / went] near being run over by a taxi.

He [nearly / barely / narrowly] escaped from being run over by a taxi.

II. Sentence Structure

1. I enjoy _____ a walk whenever I have some free time.
   (A) take (B) taking
   (C) to take (D) to have taken

2. The country gave up _____ developing countries.
   (A) to help (B) to have helped
   (C) being helped (D) helping

3. Some applicants are capable _____ English and Chinese.
   (A) to speak (B) of speaking
   (C) speaking (D) spoken

4. He objected to _____ the doctor's direction.
   (A) follow (B) be following
   (C) be followed (D) following

5. These products can be ordered by _____ our toll-free number.
   (A) dial (B) dialing
   (C) to dial (D) to have been dialed

6. Our company has a large advertising department which is responsible for advertising and _____ our goods.
   (A) marketing (B) market
   (C) marketed (D) markets

7. Employees who are used to _____ written feedback from their managers will find it difficult to deal with verbal feedback.
   (A) get (B) gotten
   (C) have gotten (D) getting

연구 및 정답

1. (B) enjoy는 동명사를 목적어로 취한다.
2. (D) give up은 동명사를 목적어로 취한다.
3. (B) be capable of -ing.
4. (D) object to -ing.
5. (B) 전치사 -ing.
6. (A) 전치사 -ing and -ing 병렬구조.
7. (D) be used to + 동사원형: -하는데 이용되다, be used to +ing: -에 익숙하다.

1. I can't afford _____ a new car.
   (A) buy (B) to buy
   (C) buying (D) bought

2. They are considering _____ to Atlanta.
   (A) move (B) to move
   (C) moving (D) will move

3. My son is not very good at _____ yet.
   (A) drive (B) to drive
   (C) driving (D) will drive

4. Nike has announced that it is going to discontinue _____ its unprofitable swimwear.
   (A) make (B) to make
   (C) made (D) making

5. You must be aware that _____ any kind of contracts should be done very carefully.
   (A) signing (B) sign
   (C) signature (D) to signing

6. He has suggested _____ a bid for our production plant in Vietnam.
   (A) to make (B) making
   (C) to making (D) that make

7. I deeply regret _____ my temper during the negotiations.
   (A) to lose (B) loses
   (C) losing (D) lost

연구 및 정답

1. (B) can't afford to부정사: 할 여유가 없다.
2. (C) consider-ing, consider는 미래의 의미를 지니지만 예외임.
3. (C) 전치사 -ing.
4. (D) discontinue -ing.
5. (A) 주어가 필요.
6. (B) suggest-ing.
7. (C) regret+to동사원형: 하게 되어 유감이다, regret+ing: 한 것을 후회하다.

1. Kevin was scolded for _____ on time.
   (A) not to come (B) to not come
   (C) not coming (D) coming not

2. _____ tends to weaken as we grow old.
   (A) We hearing (B) We to hear
   (C) Our hearing (D) Our to hear

3. He was awakened _____.
   (A) by the dog bark (B) by the dog to bark
   (C) by the dog's to bark (D) by the dog's barking

4. We appreciate _____ our friends last night.
   (A) you help (B) you to help
   (C) your to help (D) your helping

5. We regret _____ you he died as a consequence of his injuries.
   (A) inform (B) informing
   (C) to inform (D) to have informed

6. I can't remember _____ to the hospital after I fell down in the classroom.
   (A) to take (B) to be taken
   (C) taking (D) being taken

7. Did you have _____ my office?
   (A) difficulty finding (B) difficulty to find
   (C) difficulties finding (D) difficulties to find

연구 및 정답

1. (C) 전치사 not, never -ing.
2. (C) 동명사의 의미상 주어는 소유격을 원칙.
3. (D) by the dog's barking.
4. (D) appreciate -ing.
5. (C) regret to부정사: -하게 되어서 유감이다.
6. (D) remember -ing: 한 것을 기억하다의 수동 구문.
7. (A) have difficulty (in) -ing.

Ⅲ. Grammar Practice

1. Bill Gates earned <u>his</u>(A) <u>success</u>(B) by <u>work</u>(C) very <u>hard.</u>(D)

2. <u>A car</u>(A) <u>burns</u>(B) <u>gasoline</u>(C) to keep <u>to run</u>(D).

3. <u>It</u>(A) <u>is not</u>(B) <u>easy</u>(C) to quit <u>to smoke</u>(D).

4. Today, <u>people</u>(A) think <u>much</u>(B) of <u>spend</u>(C) time with <u>their</u>(D) family.

5. <u>Him</u>(A) not agreeing <u>to accept</u>(B) the proposals <u>outlined</u>(C) by the committee <u>is baffling</u>(D).

6. <u>Tom calling</u>(A) Marie made <u>her</u>(B) angry, <u>so</u>(C) she <u>hung up</u>(D) on him.

7. <u>The mountains</u>(A) and canyons <u>of</u>(B) Utah are <u>excellent</u>(C) places for hunting and <u>to fish</u>(D).

연구 및 정답

1. (C) 전치사 -ing.
2. (D) keep -ing.
3. (D) quit -ing.
4. (C) 전치사 -ing.
5. (A) 동명사의 의미상의 주어는 소유격이 원칙임.
6. (A) calling의 의미상 주어 Tom's.
7. (D) 전치사 -ing + -ing 병렬구조.

1. Acquire (A) education is the principal way of gaining status in a culture that generally stresses (B) achievement (C), skillfulness, and upward (D) mobility.

2. Cowboys in movies (A) never come to have any (B) trouble to drawing (C) guns out (D) of their holsters.

3. Some of the questions that scholars ask seem (A) to the world to be scarcely (B) worth to ask (C), let alone (D) answering.

4. Banks are differentiated (A) from other financial institutions (B) by their principal functions (C) of accepting deposits and to make loans (D).

5. A major issue (A) at the Constitutional Convention of 1787 was the decision (B) concerning the manner (C) of election (D) the President.

6. When (A) and by whom (B) the islands of the West Indies were first settled is a matter of debating (C) among (D) archaeologists.

7. Long (A) before the dawn (B) of recorded (C) history humans celebrated to harvest (D) their crops.

연구 및 정답

1. (A) 문맥상 Acquire education이 주어가 되어야 한다. Acquire → Acquiring.
2. (C) have trouble (in) -ing.
3. (C) be worth -ing.
4. (D) 전치사 of의 목적어가 되어야 한다. to make → making.
5. (D) 다음에 목적어(the President)가 있으므로 D를 동사적 성질을 지니고 있는 electing으로 고침.
6. (C) 다음에 목적어가 없으므로 동사적 성질을 지니고 있는 동명사는 부적합하다.
   debating → debate.
7. (D) 동사 celebrated는 동명사를 목적어로 취한다.

Ⅳ. Vocabulary

※ Choose the one which has the closest meaning with the underlined part.

1. As a performer, Martha Graham had a <u>commanding</u> personality and an intensity that captivated audience.
   (A) outgoing (B) extravagant
   (C) forceful (D) sympathetic

2. Clark Gable gave a <u>comic</u> performance in the movie *It Happened One Night*.
   (A) sophisticated (B) clever
   (C) discreet (D) funny

3. In ancient times the <u>custom</u> of shaking hands served to transfer power or authority.
   (A) practice (B) folklore
   (C) culture (D) doctrine

4. Habits can be <u>consciously</u> strengthened, as when a student of the violin practices.
   (A) conveniently (B) lastingly
   (C) intentionally (D) robustly

5. Horace Greeley sponsored several project in <u>communal</u> living, including the colony named for him at Greeley, Colorado.
   (A) cooperative (B) adult
   (C) apartment (D) luxurious

6. At the end of the last ice age, the Earth's <u>climate</u> began to change.
   (A) biological balance (B) rotation
   (C) weather condition (D) geography

7. In a formal paper it is <u>compulsory</u> to use footnotes each time a source is quoted.
   (A) mandatory (B) acceptable
   (C) satisfactory (D) sensible

연구

1. command: bid, power, control.
2. comical: amusing, funny, humorous.
3. custom: tradition, habit, practice.
4. conscious: realizing, sensitive, aware.
5. communal: public, shared, general
7. compulsory: compelled, required, necessary.

정답

1. C 2. D 3. A 4. C 5. A 6. C 7. A

1. An underlying assumption in most cultures is that both the individual and society will profit from an excellent educational system.
   (A) unproven (B) implicit (C) unnerving (D) impressive

2. During the Civil War, the states fought many desperate battles to uphold their asserted right to secede from the Union.
   (A) improve (B) preserve
   (C) detect (D) supply

3. Some children display an unquenchable curiosity about every new thing they encounter.
   (A) insatiable (B) inherent
   (C) indiscriminate (D) incredible

4. Lipstick is probably the most ubiquitous kind of make-up.
   (A) universal (B) alluring
   (C) indelible (D) admired

5. Pound for pound, the leopard is unequivocally the most powerful of Africa's predators.
   (A) a long way from (B) different from
   (C) astonishingly (D) definitely

6. Cases of chronic diabetes were almost unheard-of in the 1920's.
   (A) eradicated (B) documented
   (C) unbearable (D) unknown

7. Urban renewal programs strive to upgrade areas that are becoming slums.
   (A) reproach (B) improve (C) fortify (D) uproot

연구

1. underlying: fundamental, essential, implicit.
2. uphold: support, sustain, maintain, preserve.
3. unquenchable; very greedy, insatiable.
4. ubiquitous: universal.
5. unequivocal: clear, definite.
6. unheard-of: unknown.
7. upgrade: improve, progress, mend, advance.

정답

1. B 2. B 3. A 4. A 5. D 6. D 7. B

CHAPTER 10

PARTICIPLE

I. Grammar Focus

A. 분사의 의미와 용법

- a **sleeping** baby — **fallen** leaves
  an exciting story — a **broken** desk
- a **dancing** girl
  The only car **repaired** by that mechanic is mine.
- We were **exhausted.**
  I found him **surrounded** by his children.

(1) 분사는
- 현재분사 (자동사) : 진행의 의미
- (타동사) : 능동의 의미
- 과거분사 (자동사) : 완료된 동작의 상태
- (타동사) : 수동의 의미

a **smoking** man; a man who **is smoking.** (자동사)

a **loving** son; a son who **loves** his parents. (타동사)

a **returned** soldier; soldier who **have returned.** (자동사)

a **murdered** man; a man who **is murdered.** (타동사)

(2) 한정적 용법

명사 수식의 분사로서, 보어·목적어·부사(구) 등이 수반되면 반드시 뒤에서 수식 (단, 대명사도 반드시 뒤에서 수식)

The boy **singing by the gate** is my brother.

The man **writing the novel** is my friend.

Of those **invited** only a few came to the party.

(3) 서술적 용법

보어로서 사용되는 분사로서, 주격보어와 목적격 보어

He sat **surrounded** by his children. (주격보어)

The children walked **singing** merrily. (주격보어)

I don't like such subjects **discussed.** (목적격보어)

I saw some boys **playing** catch on the playground. (목적격보어)

Key Point 1

감정동사가 분사의 종류 결정

사람		사물	
	bored		boring
	satisfied		satisfying
	interested		interesting
	excited		exciting
	amused		amusing

She is **surprising** at the news. (X)
She is **surprised** at the news. (O)
It is **pleasant** for her to pass the test. (O)
It is **pleased** for her to pass the test. (X)

Key Point 2

the + 분사 - 복수보통명사(~하는 사람들), 추상명사(~것, 일)

The dying(=dying people) were lying about the field.

The wounded(=wounded people) were carried to the hospital.
cf.) the deceased(고인), the accused(피고인),

The unknown has a mysterious attraction.(미지의 것)

Key Point 3

"명사-ed"의 형용사는 "~을 가진"의 뜻으로 사용

a **red-haired** boy(빨간 머리의 소년)
a **hot-tempered** woman(성미가 급한 여인)
a **one-legged** soldier(다리가 하나인 병사)

Key Point 4

한정적 용법의 "~ed"는 "very"로 수식

a **very worried** look.

She is a **very celebrated** pianist.
cf.) She was **much worried**.

B. 분사 구문의 시제와 의미

Living near his house, I often see him.

Having done my task, I am free.

Looking out of the window, I saw a stranger.

Not knowing what to say, I kept silent.

Turning to the left, you will find the school.

Admitting what you say, I still don't believe it.

The train starts at six, **arriving in Seoul at ten**.

(1) 분사 구문의 시제- 단순형(동사원형+ing) : 주절의 시제와 일치
완료형(Having p.p) : 주절보다 하나 앞선 시제

Being ill, (=As he was ill) he **was** confined to his room.

Having finished (=After he had finished) his work, he **went** out.

(2) 분사구문의 의미

- 시간(=when, while, after, etc)

  Left to herself, she began to weep. (=When she was left to herself,…)
- 이유(=as, since, because, etc)

  Overcome with surprise, he was unable to speak.

  (=As he was overcome with surprise,…)
- 조건(=if…)

  The poison, **used in a small quantity**, will be a medicine.

  (=The poison, if it is used in small quantity,…)
- 양보(=Though…, even if…)

  Admitting what you say, you are still in the wrong. (=Though I (we) admit…)
- 부대상황(=…, and…)

  Walking slowly, I approached the scene. (=I walked slowly and approached…)

C. 독립 분사 구문

- **Weather permitting**, we shall take a walk.

  This work done, he took a rest then.
- **Strictly speaking**, this sentence is not grammatical.

  Taking all things into consideration, he is a gentleman.

(1) 독립 분사구문

분사의 의미상 주어가 주절의 주어와 다르기 때문에 의미상 주어(주격)이 사용되는 경우를 말한다.

Nobody having any more to say, the committee broke up. (Nobody≠the committee)

It being very cold, we kept staying at home. (It≠we)

(2) 무인칭 독립 분사 구문

독립 분사구문의 의미상주어가 일반인(we, they, you…)일 경우 주로 관용적 표현.

- strictly speaking 엄격히 말하면(=if we speak strictly)
- generally speaking 일반적으로 말하면
- judging from~ ~으로 판단하면
- taking all things into consideration 만사를 고려한다면
- considering~ ~을 고려한다면

D. 분사구문의 주의할 용법

- **Not having received an answer**, I wrote him again.
- **There being much noise**, I couldn't hear his voice.
- **Standing as it does on a hill**, the church commands a fine view.
- He was lying on the sofa, **with his eyes closed**.

(1) 분사구문의 부정

분사 앞에 not, never를 둠으로써 부정한다.

Not knowing what to say, I kept silent.

Never having been to America, I was at a loss then.

(2) There(Here) 분사구문

분사 앞에 There(Here)를 반드시 위치한다.

There being nothing more to do, we continued chatting.

Here being much money in his pocket, he could buy much furniture.

(3) 분사구문의 강조용법

분사구문 - 현재분사(~ing) + as + S + do동사

과거분사(~ed) + as + S + be동사

→ (해석) 사실, 그렇게

Living **as I do** remote from the town, I have few visitors.

Occurring **as it did** only once a year, I regarded it as a special case.

Situated **as it is** on the hill, the house commands a fine view.

(4) 부대상황의 부사구

"with+명사+분사·형용사·전치사"의 형태로 "~하면서, ~한 채로"로 해석된다.

She stood there **with her hair waving** in the wood.

She took a walk **with her dog following** behind her.

He was sitting over there **with his arms folded.**

She was lying on the mat **with her mouth open.**

Tom was playing tennis **with his hat on.**

II. Sentence Structure

1. That's a very _____ movie.
   (A) to be interested (B) interested
   (C) interesting (D) interest

2. Several employees _____ at the firm were seriously injured.
   (A) work (B) working
   (C) to work (D) worked

3. When he heard the good news, he was _____.
   (A) excitement (B) exciting
   (C) to excite (D) excited

4. There will be an _____ remark of the president.
   (A) open (B) openly
   (C) opening (D) opened

5. People _____ the computer training course can become members.
   (A) joining (B) joined
   (C) to have joined (D) who has joined

6. Peterson is well known as a _____ man in the personnel department.
   (A) hard-work (B) worked hard
   (C) hard-working (D) working hardly

7. Ms. Miller heard some _____ news from her friend who lives in Italy.
   (A) exciting (B) excited
   (C) excitement (D) more excited

연구 및 정답

1. (C) 감정을 느끼면 p.p, 그 감정을 주면 ~ing.
2. (B) 능동의 형용사는 -ing.
3. (D) 감정을 느끼면 p.p(주로 사람).
4. (C) opening remark 개회사.
5. (A) 능동의 형용사는 -ing.
6. (C) 능동의 형용사는 -ing.
7. (A) 감정을 주면 ~ing.

1. He spoke for a long time and his speech was very _____.
   (A) boring (B) bored
   (C) bore (D) boredom

2. _____ the work, I went to the movies.
   (A) Finishing (B) Being finished
   (C) Finished (D) Having finished

3. The first commercial film _____ in California was completed in 1907.
   (A) made (B) making
   (C) to make (D) was made

4. I thought I saw professor Davis _____ in the library last night.
   (A) working (B) to work
   (C) works (D) worked

5. _____ in all parts of the state, pines are the most common tree in Georgia.
   (A) Found (B) Finding them
   (C) To find them (D) They are found

6. He had his temperature _____ in the hospital.
   (A) taking (B) to take
   (C) taken (D) take

7. Please provide your _____ time of arrival when you reply.
   (A) estimate (B) estimating
   (C) estimated (D) estimation

연구 및 정답

1. (A) 지루한 연설, 지루함을 주니까 -ing.
2. (D) 일이 끝난 것은 더 과거 그러므로 완료 분사 구조(having pp).
3. (A) film (which was) made.
4. (A) 지각동사 + O + 동사원형(-ing).
5. (A) As they are found; (As they are) found.
6. (C) 온도를 재는 주체는 사람, 온도는 객체 pp.
7. (C) 시간을 측정하는 사람은 -ing(능동), 시간은 수동.

1. He lay on a straw mat with his _____.
   (A) closed eyes and his mouth open
   (B) eyes closed and his open mouth
   (C) closed eyes and open his mouth
   (D) eyes closed and his mouth open

2. _____, he washed the cup and put it away.
   (A) Having drank the coffee
   (B) Drinking the coffee
   (C) Having drunk the coffee
   (D) After drank the coffee

3. Written in great haste, _____.
   (A) the book is full of errors
   (B) there are plenty of errors in the report
   (C) we found several mistakes in his letter
   (D) Jim made a lot of mistakes in the report

4. _____ in an atmosphere of rigid New England Puritanism, Harriet Beecher Stowe demonstrated an interest in theology at a young age.
   (A) Raise her
   (B) Raised
   (C) Raising
   (D) She was raised

5. The tail of a meteor is highly perishable, _____ for just a few seconds.
   (A) lasts
   (B) lasting
   (C) lasted
   (D) and lasting

6. An expensive book _____ to his club is lost.
   (A) belong
   (B) belongs
   (C) belonging
   (D) belonged

7. Upon hearing the bell ring, _____.
   (A) the students' departure was hasty
   (B) our departure was hasty
   (C) we departed hastily
   (D) the classroom was filled immediately

연구 및 정답

1. (D) with + 목적어 + 분사 (형용사, 부사, 전치사) : 분사구문, 부대상황 (-하면서).
2. (C) 분사구문의 시점이 주절의 시점을 앞서므로 완료형태 (having p.p)가 요구된다.
3. (A) (Having been) written 이 주어가 곧 주절의 주어이다.
4. (B) raise는 타동사이며 목적어를 필요로 한다. 본문에는 목적어가 없기 때문에 과거분사가 요구된다.
5. (B) perishable and lasts → perishable, lasting for ~.
6. (C) An expensive book which belongs [belonging] to ~.
7. (C) Upon ~ ring 하는 주체가 사람이므로 주절의 주어는 사람이어야 한다.

Ⅲ. Grammar Practice

1. Walking (A) along (B) the bridge, I (C) heard my name calling (D).

2. My parents are in (A) a small country (B) town, lived (C) a peaceful life (D).

3. Broad speaking (A), the social studies deal with (B) man's (C) relationship to (D) other men.

4. A red-hair (A) boy is needed (B) to play the part (C) of Alfred in this (D) new comedy.

5. The average (A) age of the Mediterranean (B) olive trees grow (C) today is two hundred years (D).

6. Knowing not (A) the language and having no (B) friends in the country, he found it (C) impossible to get a job (D).

7. Beverly Hills, surrounding (A) by the city of Los Angeles, is famous for (B) its luxurious (C) home and many exclusive shops (D).

연구 및 정답

1. (D) 목적보어와 목적어의 관계가 수동 called.
2. (C) 분사구문의 연속동작이면서 능동 living.
3. (A) 무인칭 독립 분사 구문. If we speak broadly; Broadly Speaking.
4. (A) 유사 분사, 명사+ed 분사처럼 사용.
5. (C) trees를 수식하는 자동사로 진행의 의미를 지니는 분사가 필요.
6. (A) 분사의 부정은 분사 앞에.
7. (A) as it is surrounded ~.

1. Those interesting (A) in signing up (B) for the class should (C) do so (D) immediately.

2. Hiawatha was a reformer (A), interesting (B) in ending (C) war and promoting universal (D) peace among the Iroquois tribes.

3. Shocking (A) at the news, his father said (B) nothing (C) and fell (D) down.

4. Scientists (A) still can't find (B) any convinced (C) link between intelligence and the quantity (D) or quality of brain cells.

5. Romanticists (A) show life as being (B) more emotionally excited and satisfying (C) than it normally (D) is.

6. We can supplement our own ideas with (A) information and data (B) gathering (C) from our reading, our observation, and so forth (D).

7. The loser team (A) protested that they (B) had not been given impartial treatment (C) by (D) the officials.

연구 및 정답

1. (A) Those who are interested in ~.
2. (B) (who was) interested in ~.
3. (A) As he was shocked ~.
4. (C) convincing link.
5. (C) emotionally exciting and satisfying 병렬구조.
6. (C) data which was gathered ~.
7. (A) 진 팀은 lost team.

Ⅳ. Vocabulary

※ Choose the one which has the closest meaning with the underlined part.

1. Laster technology has enhanced the precision of many surgical.
   (A) cost (B) accuracy
   (C) cleanliness (D) innovation
2. In the Pacific Northwest, climate and topography vary, so do the species the prevail in the forests.
   (A) rebuild (B) invade
   (C) dominate (D) tend
3. Lasers are often the preferred tools of surgeons in the modern operating room.
   (A) sole (B) best
   (C) favored (D) required
4. Students learning about how life began on Earth may be presented with the puzzling question, "Which came first, the chicken or the egg?"
   (A) pressing (B) perplexing
   (C) patronizing (D) penetrating
5. Shellac varnish is purified lac that is secreted by scale insects.
   (A) refined (B) starchy
   (C) resilient (D) virtuous
6. Frank Lloyd Wright's early writing on architecture was prophetic of the development that eventually produced a universal style.
   (A) indicative (B) predictive
   (C) demonstrative (D) imitative
7. Prior to the use of nickel in 1835, spoons were made exclusively of silver or pewter.
   (A) Before (B) In
   (C) At the time of (D) Due to

연구

1. precise: exact, accurate, definite, careful.
2. prevail: dominate, surpass, outweigh.
3. prefer: choose, favor, rather, desire.
4. puzzle: perplexity, confusion, dilemma, bewilderment.
5. purify: cleanse, clear, refine, filter.
6. prophesy: predict, foretell, forecast, foresee.
7. prior: earlier, before, previous, former.

정답

1. B 2. C 3. C 4. B 5. A 6. B 7. A

1. Iron occurs in combination with numerous other elements.
   (A) expands (B) melts
   (C) exists (D) deteriorates

2. Regional planning deals with proposals concerning outlying communities and highways as well as with urban affairs.
   (A) outlandish (B) exclusive
   (C) exempted (D) remote

3. The first major outburst of musical creativity in the United States occurred at the end of the nineteenth century.
   (A) surge (B) round
   (C) outcome (D) performance

4. During the medieval epoch, the sciences were considered to be based on the occult.
   (A) theoretical (B) anthropological
   (C) fundamental (D) supernatural

5. Sequoya, a Native American who was born about 1770, formed an alphabet of eighty-six letters that enabled him to put the oral Cherokee language into writing.
   (A) secret (B) complex
   (C) spoken (D) ancient

6. The Milky Way is among the most outstanding spectacles in the heavens.
   (A) persistent (B) threatening
   (C) remarkable (D) stable

7. Choking occurs when the flow of air to the lungs is obstructed.
   (A) restructured (B) rejected
   (C) vented (D) blocked

연구

1. occur: happen, take place, transpire, come about.
2. outlying: remote, external, outer.
3. outburst: eruption, outbreak, ejection, surge.
4. occult: mysterious, supernatural, secret, esoteric.
5. oral: spoken, voiced, verbal, uttered.
6. outstanding: well-known, prominent, conspicuous, eminent.
7. obstruct: block, hinder, clog, bar, impede, delay.

정답

1. C 2. D 3. A 4. D 5. C 6. C 7. D

CHAPTER 11

PREPOSITION

I. Grammar Focus

A. 전치사 다음에는 꼭 명사를!

1. 전치사 + 일반 명사 (on the internet)
2. 전치사 + 대명사 목적격 (between you and me)
3. 전치사 + 동명사 (by-ing, without -ing)
4. 전치사 + 전명구 (from around the world, except in the room)

There are many people in the stadium.

He came to the stadium with her.

They ate hamburgers before watching the game.

B. ~분야(in)

: 증가/감소 in, in the sales department, advances in, experience in, be busy in ~ing, have difficulty in ~ing, assist in ~ing/assist with 명사, spend 시간/돈 in/on ~ing,

~아래/~중

: under management, ~supervision, control, construction, development, consideration

~로서 : as

with/without : without having to, without exceptions,
with a balance of, with the aim of, problem with

through the use of, through arbitration

by ~ing, by 숫자 : ~만큼

at: 속도, 가격, 주소, 번호, 홈피...

용도, 대상 : for sale, for visitors

on: on the rise/the wane, on one's way to

beyond expectation, beyond control

concern over, dispute over

information on/ about

regardless of =notwithstanding

C. 명사 of 명사

- 주격: a recent outbreak of SARS
- 소유격: the leg of this desk
- 목적격: the development of this city
- 동격: the aim of fulfilling his job

D. 양보의 전치사(despite, in spite of, with all, for all)

In spite of his hard work, he couldn't finish the project by the deadline.

Customers are satisfied with the products despite the high award.

E. 이유의 전치사(because of, due to, owing to, thanks to)

Because of the heavy rain, the game was canceled.

F. 시점 Vs. 기간의 전치사

(1) by Vs. until "~할 때 까지"(시점)

: by는 - 일회적/단발성 동작 일 때(submit, return, receive, inform),
until은 -지속적 일 때(stay, wait, continue, remain, last 등)

(2) for Vs. during "~하는 동안" (기간)

: for+숫자, during+기간명사

(3) throughout Vs. over (기간)

: throughout (처음부터 끝까지 계속) -throughout the conference
over(어떤 기간에 걸쳐서 쭉 계속) -over the past three years
*over대신, in, for등도 가능

(4) within Vs. in

: within~이내에(능력, 기간, 범위)
in+시간:~시간 후에, in+물리적 장소
*within +기간, by+시점

(5) before=prior to, after=following

G. 시간의 전치사

- at+정확시각
- on+요일, 날짜
- in+오전, 오후, 저녁, 달, 계절, 세기,

* 다음은 전치사(in, on) 안 씀. -부사로 쓰이기 때문
last~, this~, next~, yesterday, today, tomorrow, tonight

H. 장소 전치사 (동작이 없을 때)

at, in, on, over, under, above, below, beside, between/among, behind,

I. 장소 전치사 (동작 있을 때)

for/ toward, to, into, out of, from, through, around/ round, along,
cross/ across, beyond /within, up/ down, over/under,

J. ~을 제외하고

except (직설법, 현재 있는 것)~을 제외하고(문장 맨 앞에는 잘 쓰지 않음)

*except=but=except for = excepting 모두 전치사임.

*except that(when) + S + V, S + V

*barring(가정법, 미래에 있을 것)~을 제외 한다면 = but for=without

*excluding+명사, including~을 포함하여

K. 기타 전치사

(1) ~에 관하여

: concerning, regarding, about, as to/ as for, with(in) regard(respect, reference) to

(2) by+교통, 통신 수단

(3) ~외에도 : besides, in addition to, apart from, aside from, on top of, as well as

*besides, moreover, in addition, as well은 부사도 가능

II. Sentence Structure

1. We have to finish the annual report _____ November 25.
   (A) by (B) in
   (C) until (D) at

2. He is in charge _____ the analysis of all financial affairs.
   (A) for (B) with
   (C) of (D) in

3. _____ meeting today, we will meet tomorrow to discuss the proposal.
   (A) However (B) For
   (C) Due to (D) Instead of

4. The museum will remain open _____ 10 o'clock in July and August.
   (A) by (B) during
   (C) until (D) for

5. The express bus leaves from the terminal every hour _____ the hour.
   (A) by (B) for
   (C) from (D) on

6. He had to work overtime in December _____ the heavy demand for summer catalogs.
   (A) because (B) unless
   (C) because of (D) since

7. _____ a kangaroo, the opossum carries its babies in a pouch.
   (A) It is (B) When
   (C) As (D) Like

연구 및 정답

1. (A) 완료의 전치사 by, 계속의 전치사 until.
2. (C) be in charge of ~을 담당하고 있다.
3. (D) Instead of 대신에.
4. (C) 계속의 전치사 until.
5. (D) on the hour 정시에.
6. (C) because S + V, because of + 명사.
7. (D) Like ~처럼(전치사).

1. "How do I write my composition?" "Write your composition _____ ink."
   (A) in (B) with
   (C) by (D) on

2. "How are you going?" "We are going _____ boat."
   (A) in (B) with
   (C) on (D) by

3. China lies _____ the west of Korea.
   (A) in (B) on
   (C) to (D) by

4. Dr. Jones is an authority _____ urban planning.
   (A) in (B) of
   (C) on (D) with

5. I haven't seen him _____ ages.
   (A) with (B) for
   (C) during (D) until

6. You can make payments _____ regular business hours on Tuesday and Thursday.
   (A) for (B) during
   (C) except (D) while

7. _____ all our efforts to save the school, the authorities decided to close it.
   (A) Once (B) Because of
   (C) Unless (D) Despite

연구 및 정답

1. (A) 재료의 전치사 in.
2. (D) by + 교통수단.
3. (C) 지명을 표시할 경우, ~안에 있을 경우 전치사 in, 인접한 경우 전치사 on, ~향해서. 있을 경우 전치사 to를 각각 사용한다.
4. (B) an authority of ~의 권위자.
5. (B) for ages 오랫동안.
6. (B) during + 기간명사 (cf. for + 숫자).
7. (D) Despite + 명사, ~에도 불구하고.

1. High-Quality Health Care & Restoration has been providing excellent services _____ over twenty years.
   (A) among (B) with
   (C) for (D) since

2. According to a recent study, smoking rates have been increasing _____ women.
   (A) between (B) among
   (C) with (D) on

3. Only people with ID cards can pass _____ the main gate.
   (A) to (B) among
   (C) below (D) through

4. You can increase your energy _____ taking a short nap.
   (A) at (B) by
   (C) for (D) with

5. You will be amazed _____ the speed and power of this new laptop.
   (A) at (B) from
   (C) for (D) with

6. _____ event coordinator, Ms. Parker is supposed to select a venue for the workshop.
   (A) Of (B) As
   (C) About (D) On

7. Management responded favorably to the prospective employees' concerns _____ the benefits package.
   (A) regard (B) regards
   (C) regarded (D) regarding

연구 및 정답

1. (C) for + 숫자.
2. (B) between +둘 사이, among + 셋 이상 사이.
3. (D) through 관통의 전치사.
4. (B) by -ing 함으로써.
5. (A) be amazed at ~에 놀라다.
6. (B) As 자격, 신분의 as.
7. (D) regarding 분사형 전치사.

III. Grammar Practice

1. Abraham Lincoln was born in February 12, 1809 in Kentucky.
   (A: was, B: born, C: in, D: in)

2. Bees fly to flower to flower for food.
   (A: Bees, B: fly, C: to, D: food)

3. Benjamin Franklin was famous of his inventions.
   (A: was, B: of, C: his, D: inventions)

4. Amelia Earhart crossed the Atlantic Ocean with airplane.
   (A: crossed, B: the, C: with, D: airplane)

5. Many people left their own countries and came America to live.
   (A: Many, B: their, C: came America, D: to live)

6. There are three kinds matter : solid, liquid, and gas.
   (A: are, B: three, C: kinds matter, D: solid)

7. John F. Kennedy gave to Americans hope for the future.
   (A: to Americans, B: for, C: the, D: future)

연구 및 정답

1. (C) 특정 날짜 앞에 on.
2. (C) from ~ to.
3. (B) be famous for ~ 로 유명하다.
4. (C) by plane.
5. (C) come 은 자동사, 자동사 +전치사+목적어.
6. (C) three kinds of matter.
7. (A) give는 수여동사이므로 바로 목적어(사람)를 받는다.

1. Millions years ago, horses had four toes on each front foot.
   A B C D

2. People are afraid for sharks, but they usually do not know very much about them.
   A B C D

3. Cowboys usually wear on hats, boots, and gloves.
   A B C D

4. Don't worry! I will wait for you by you come back.
   A B C D

5. The president has been committed to expanding the company within the last 10 years.
   A B C D

6. We assure you that you will receive the finished products until 24 hours of your order.
   A B C D

7. The university students' grades are regarded on confidential information in Korea.
   A B C D

연구 및 정답

1. (A) Millions of ~ 수백만년의.
2. (A) be afraid of.
3. (C) wear는 타동사이므로 전치사 불필요.
4. (D) 계속의 의미 until.
5. (C) for the last 10 years.
6. (C) 24시간 이내에 within.
7. (B) be regarded as.

IV. Vocabulary

※ Choose the one which has the closest meaning with the underlined part.

1. A great number of cultures have assigned high status to the elderly.
   (A) aged (B) educated
   (C) religious leaders (D) father's family
2. In swimming, a more exact coordination of muscles is required than in other sports.
   (A) a swifter (B) a more precise
   (C) a more automatic (D) an easier
3. Two composers having very similar personalities but living in two different epochs would inevitably produce music of two different styles.
   (A) cultures (B) periods of history
   (C) sets of financial circumstances (D) countries
4. In 1979, a committee of the World Meteorological Organization sanctioned a proposal that hurricanes not be named exclusively of women.
   (A) primarily (B) alphabetically
   (C) solely (D) arbitrarily
5. Learning to dance requires an elemental understanding of rhythm and movement.
   (A) a basic (B) a charitable
   (C) a trifling (D) a material
6. Babe Didrikson Zaharias excelled in basketball, baseball, and track in her youth and later became a champion golfer.
   (A) practiced (B) taught
   (C) was interested in (D) was outstanding in
7. Learning occurs most efficiently if the student is ready to learn.
   (A) tirelessly (B) effusively
   (C) effectively (D) compulsively

연구

1. elderly: old, aged.
2. exact: correct, precise, strict.
3. epoch: period, age, era.
4. exclusively: solely.
5. elemental: simple, primitive, basic.
6. excel: outstrip, transcend, exceed, surpass.
7. efficient: capable, competent, effective.

정답

1. A 2. B 3. B 4. C 5. A 6. D 7. C

1. The habitat of an animal should be large enough to yield <u>a copious</u> supply of food.
   (A) a solid (B) an indefinite
   (C) a plentiful (D) an elaborate

2. An early form of softball originated in 1895, when a Minneapolis fire fighter decided to provide a simple and inexpensive outlet for his <u>colleagues</u>.
   (A) fellow workers (B) friends and family
   (C) university (D) pets

3. Our Sun is <u>a commonplace</u> star.
   (A) an average (B) a nearby
   (C) a centrally located (D) an unusually bright

4. Some people believe the aloe plant has <u>curative</u> properties.
   (A) magical (B) organic
   (C) superior (D) healing

5. The skin of a shock victim is often <u>clammy</u>.
   (A) feverish (B) without feeling
   (C) cold and slightly damp (D) pale and easily bruised

6. Honey guides, or indicator birds, <u>collaborate</u> with honey badgers in seeking out bee colonies.
   (A) work together (B) travel north
   (C) live (D) compete

7. Because of its odd mannerisms, the praying mantis has always <u>intrigued</u> human beings.
   (A) fascinated (B) aggravated
   (C) offended (D) terrified

연구

1. copious: plentiful, abundant, ample.
2. colleague: associate, buddy, companion, comrade.
3. commonplace ordinary, average.
4. curative: healing
5. clammy: cold and damp, sweaty.
6. collaborate: cooperate, work together.
7. intrigue: fascinate, plot, scheme, conspiracy.

정답

1. C 2. A 3. A 4. D 5. C 6. A 7. A

CHAPTER 12

CONJUNCTION

I. Grammar Focus

A. 등위접속사와 상관접속사

1. 등위접속사의 종류 : and, but(=yet), or

All employees **and** their families are invited to the company picnic.

The book is boring **but(yet)** informative.

Amy enjoys reading a book in the morning **or** at night.

2. 특성

(1) 등위접속사의 특성

앞뒤로 동일구조를 갖는다(병렬/ 등위 구조), 동일요소는 생략가능하기 때문.

(2) S+V , so/for S+V : 생략 불가

(3) and, but(=yet), or, so, for 문두에 올 수 없다.

* 3개 이상 나열 시 : 명사, 명사, and 명사

3. A and B +복수동사

A but B + B에 일치하는 동사 (근접원리)

A or B + B에 일치하는 동사 (근접원리)

4. 상관접속사의 수의일치

단/ 복수 단원 참고

Both the lobby **and** the main hall require extensive renovations.

Either you **or** he is responsible for the accident.

He **as well as** you plans to make a speech in front of the audience.

B. 명사절 접속사

1. 명사절이란? 절(주어+동사)이 문장에서 S, O, C로 사용되는 것.

* 4가지 패턴을 숙지할 것.

(1) 문장의 주어자리에 올 때.

That he talked about it to reporters surprises me.

(2) 타동사 뒤에 올 때

Industry experts believe that the company is going bankrupt soon.

(3) 전치사 뒤에 올 때

Everything depends on whether we have enough money.

(4) 보어자리에 올 때.

Our conclusion is that this project will be successful.

2. what vs. that

- 둘 다 "~하는 것"으로 해석
- 둘 다 위의 4가지 패턴 모두 가능
- 뒷문장이 완전하면 that이 정답이지만, 뒷문장이 불완전하면 what이 정답.

3. if vs. whether

- 둘 다 "~이든 아니든"으로 해석
- if 뒤에는 반드시 주어+동사, whether는 변형 가능
- if절은 타동사 뒤만 사용, whether는 4가지 패턴 모두 사용.

(1) 명사절접속사 (~인지 아닌지)

※ if, whether (명사절) 의 차이점.

whether s + v or not , whether or not s + v, whether (or not) to원형 (or not),

whether A or B (상관접속사) - 다양한 변형 가능

if s+v (or not) - 이 형태 밖에 사용하지 못함 (타동사 뒤 목적절만)

(2) 부사절접속사

if s+v : ~라면 / whether s+v : ~이든 아니든

4. 의문사=명사절접속사 (의문대명사, 의문형용사, 의문부사)

- 의문사의 종류
- 의문사의 쓰임

  ① 의문사 +(주어) + 동사

  ② 의문사 to부정사

C. 부사절 접속사의 종류

	접속사+주어+동사	전치사+명사
양보	although, though, even if, even though	despite, in spite of, with all, for all
이유	because, since, as, now that, seeing that, for	because of, due to, owing to, on account of, in view of
시간	when, while, as, as soon as before/after, until, the moment, at the time SV, SV	during
조건	if, in case, once, as long as = as far as,, provided(=providing), unless, suppose=supposing, on condition that,	in case of
목적	so that~can/may=in order that	so as to, in order to, to do
~함에 따라	according as	according to
~인 것처럼	as if, as though	like
매우~해서~하다	so~that, such~that	
복합관계사		

II. Sentence Structure

1. I turned on the air conditioner _____ the room was too hot.
   (A) although (B) however
   (C) due to (D) because

2. I am looking for a job in _____ web design or internet commerce.
   (A) neither (B) nor
   (C) either (D) other

3. _____ I arrived at the party, he had already left.
   (A) While (B) By the time
   (C) In case (D) During

4. _____ this job is very hard, many applicants applied because of the good salary.
   (A) Because (B) Although
   (C) Despite (D) Due to

5. The event is _____ popular that there will be a large crowd at the stadium.
   (A) very (B) too
   (C) more (D) so

6. Employees should contact Thomson _____ there are mistakes in their wages.
   (A) prevented from (B) only if
   (C) asking for (D) all about

7. _____ some students chose to attend university in the capital city, the majority go to university in their hometowns.
   (A) Because of (B) In spite of
   (C) While (D) Yet

연구 및 정답

1. (D) 뒤에 절이 오기 때문에 접속사가 와야 하며 내용상 이유가 정답.
2. (C) either ~ or 구문.
3. (B) By the time + S+V~ 할 때 쯤.
4. (B) 절이 오기 때문에 접속사 내용상 양보가 정답.
5. (D) so ~ that 구문.
6. (B) 조건절을 나타낸다.
7. (C) While; Whereas -하는 반면에.

1. He could not go out with her until _____.
   (A) they allowed to do so
   (B) she allowed to do so
   (C) he allowed to do so
   (D) allowed to do so

2. _____, quicksand looks like powder.
   (A) Dry
   (B) It is dry
   (C) When dry
   (D) When is it

3. Each of its atoms loses or gives off a certain amount of energy _____ substance is radiating energy.
   (A) with a
   (B) a
   (C) when is a
   (D) if a

4. Neon is said to be inert _____ does not react easily with other substances.
   (A) because of it
   (B) because it
   (C) it is because
   (D) is because it

5. _____ their nests well, but also build them well.
   (A) Not only brown thrashers protect
   (B) Protect no only brown thrashers
   (C) Brown thrashers not only protect
   (D) Not only protect brown thrashers

6. A legislative body has the power not only to pass new laws, _____ repeal laws that have been passed earlier.
   (A) to
   (B) but also to
   (C) and to
   (D) in order to

7. John is _____ that he can score points easily.
   (A) a very tall player
   (B) so tall player
   (C) so a tall player
   (D) such a tall player

연구 및 정답

1. (D) 부사절을 이끄는 접속사 다음에 S+be동사의 생략이 가능하다.
   until (he was) allowed to~. cf) though I am tired, I study. = Though tired, I study.
2. (C) 본문의 주절은 S+V 형태를 갖추고 있다. 따라서 종속절이 적합하다. When (it is) dry,
3. (D) 다음에 주어와 동사가 나타나므로 접속사가 요구된다.
4. (B) because of+명사 상당 어구 / because+S+V.
5. (C) 상관접속사 not only A but also B 구문. 이 경우 A, B는 대등한 어구이어야 한다.
6. (B) not only A but also B 구문.
7. (D) such a tall player; so tall a player.

1. He walked warily _____ he should fall.
   (A) lest (B) unless
   (C) except (D) before

2. The ship changed its course _____ there was a storm.
   (A) on account of (B) due to
   (C) because of (D) because

3. He did not get the telegram in time _____.
   (A) because it was delivered late (B) as it was delivered late
   (C) since it was late delivered (D) because of it was delivered

4. _____ people depend to such a great extent on forests, every effort must be made to preserve trees and wildlife.
   (A) How (B) That
   (C) Since (D) Which

5. Advertising is distinguished from other forms of communication _____ the advertiser pays for the message to be delivered.
   (A) in that (B) which
   (C) whereas (D) because of

6. Trumpeter Wynton Marsalis has won Grammy Awards for his recordings of _____ jazz and classical music.
   (A) also (B) together
   (C) the two (D) both

7. When they were written, many nursery rhymes were intended not for children _____ for adults.
   (A) nevertheless (B) but
   (C) instead of (D) on the other hand

연구 및 정답

1. (A) lest~should.
2. (D) 다음에 절이 나타나므로 접속사가 적합하다.
3. (A) as와 since는 formal expression에서는 문미에 사용되지 않는다.
4. (C) comma 다음에 완전한 하나의 문장을 형성하고 있으므로 그 앞은 수식요소 즉 부사절(구)이 적합하다.
5. (A) in that S+V : ~라는 점에 있어서.
6. (D) both A and B 구문.
7. (B) not A but B 구문.

Ⅲ. Grammar Practice

1. Consequently(A) sharks are heavier than water, they must swim(B) continuously(C) or they will sink to the bottom(D).

2. Meerschaum is so light(A) that will it(B) float(C) in water(D).

3. Many persons(A) once held(B) that liverworts curing(C) liver diseases(D).

4. Author(A) Sarah Orne Jewett published her(B) first story when was(C) nineteen years(D) old.

5. The hammer has been(A) used as a(B) tool since(C) the Neolithic period when was(D) invented.

6. The architect(A) must be(B) both(C) a scientist and artistic(D).

7. Rubber can be made(A) too(B) elastic that it will stretch(C) more than nine times its(D) normal length.

연구 및 정답

1. (A) 다음에 주어+동사 나오므로 A를 문장의 내용상 Because로 바꾼다.
2. (B) 접속사 + 주어 + 동사.
3. (C) that가 접속사이므로 주어+동사가 필요하다. curing → cured.
4. (C) when + S + V when she was.
5. (D) when + S + V when it was.
6. (D) both A and B 구문에서 A와 B는 동등어구이어야 한다. artistic → artist.
7. (B) so~that구문. too → so.

1. Generally alcohols are neutral compounds displaying neither acid or alkaline.
(A: Generally, B: are, C: displaying, D: or)

2. The element ruthenium is hard and brittle, and does not dissolve in either water nor acid.
(A: hard, B: does, C: in, D: nor)

3. An American is not merely confident but is ambitious and loves freedom.
(A: An American, B: not merely, C: is ambitious, D: loves)

4. The onion has both a distinctive flavor or odor.
(A: The onion, B: has, C: distinctive, D: or)

5. Not only was the Mariner spacecraft the first to fly beyond Mars, however it also survived in space well past its expected lifetime of twenty-one months.
(A: spacecraft, B: however it, C: well past, D: expected)

6. From its beginning in 1639, Newport was a haven for colonial privateers as well a major port for trade.
(A: its, B: a, C: as well, D: trade)

7. My nose as well as my ears were bleeding when the doctor was brought in.
(A: were, B: when, C: was, D: brought in)

연구 및 정답

1. (D) neither A nor B 구문.
2. (D) either A or B 구문.
3. (C) not merely(only) A but (also) B A와 B는 동일 구조.
4. (D) both A and B.
5. (B) not only A but also B.
6. (C) as well as.
7. (A) A as well as B 구조에서 수일치는 A에 일치시킴.

Ⅳ. Vocabulary

※ Choose the one which has the closest meaning with the underlined part.

1. I will mediate on your <u>precepts</u>.
   (A) power (B) glory
   (C) greatness (D) instruction

2. If there are civilizations on other planets, they are likely to be <u>radically</u> different from ours.
   (A) exactly (B) approximately
   (C) partially (D) basically

3. When bothered by other animals or humans, some species of lizard will posture <u>threateningly</u> and squirt blood from their eyes.
   (A) menacingly (B) distrustfully
   (C) fiercely (D) imprudently

4. About a <u>quarter</u> of the workers in the United States are employed in the factories.
   (A) third (B) fourth
   (C) tenth (D) fifteenth

5. Ammonia, one of the earliest known nitrogen compounds, was originally produced by distilling organic <u>materials</u>.
   (A) masses (B) fabrics
   (C) substances (D) liquids

6. Many fossil's are <u>uncovered</u> by changes in the surface of the earth.
   (A) altered (B) ruined
   (C) formed (D) revealed

7. Many people who are colorblinded cannot <u>recognize</u> different hues of red and green.
   (A) distinguish (B) reproduce
   (C) coordinate (D) recount

연구

1. precept 교훈, 훈계.
2. radically: basically. approximately 거의, 약, 대개.
3. threateningly 협박하는, 험악한. menacingly 위협적으로. impudently 뻔뻔스럽게.
5. fabrics 섬유.
6. uncover ~의 뚜껑을 열다.
7. coordinate 조정(통합)하다.

정답

1. D 2. D 3. A 4. B 5. C 6. D 7. A

1. The Depression in the United States <u>lasted</u> until the beginning of the Second World War.
   (A) was avoided (B) continued
   (C) has been restrained (D) deteriorated
2. The Women's Army Corps was <u>founded</u> in 1942.
   (A) supported (B) established
   (C) discovered (D) emphasized
3. Blue-green algae grow <u>abundantly</u> in salt marshes.
   (A) primarily (B) slowly
   (C) on plants (D) in great numbers
4. <u>Formerly</u>, in the Unites States, many nurses worked as private duty nurses rather than in hospitals.
   (A) Previously (B) Strictly
   (C) Officially (D) Periodically
5. The National Industrial Recovery Act was designed to <u>spur</u> industry.
   (A) tax (B) stimulate
   (C) censure (D) rebuke
6. Food must be <u>moist</u> in order to have taste.
   (A) appetizing (B) nutritious
   (C) damp (D) chewed
7. <u>Motivation</u> is primary factor in learning.
   (A) Memorization (B) Aptitude
   (C) Intelligence (D) Incentive

연구

1. deteriorate 타락시키다.
3. marsh 늪, 습지.
4. formerly 이전의. periodically 정기적으로.
5. spur 고무시키다.
6. appetizing 식욕을 돋구는. nutritious 영양분이 있는.
7. motivation 동기화, 자극.

정답

1. B 2. B 3. D 4. A 5. B 6. C 7. D

CHAPTER 13

RELATIVE PRONOUN

I. Grammar Focus

A. 관계대명사

	사람	사물	선행사 제한 없음
주격	who	which	that
소유격	whose	of which나 whose	없음
목적격	whom	which	that

1. Who

- This is the girl. She is a good typist.

→ This is the girl **who** is a good typist.

- A child is called an orphan. His parents are dead.

→ A child **whose** parents are dead is called an orphan.

2. Which

(1) 주격, 목적격으로 쓰일 때

- I have a book. It is very interesting.

→ I have a book **which** is very interesting.

- This is the dictionary. I bought it yesterday.

→ This is the dictionary **which** I bought yesterday.

(2) 구, 절 형용사를 선행사로 받을 때

- He wanted **to come**, **which** was impossible.
- She looks **well off**, **which** she really is not.

(3) 신분. 지위, 성격의 낱말을 선행사로 받을 때

- He is **a gentleman**, **which** his brother is not.

3. That

that은 한정용법에만 쓰이고, 계속적인 용법에는 쓸 수 없음.

that은 사물, 사람, 동물에 모두 쓰이며, 소유격이 없음.

that앞에는 전치사를 쓸 수 없음.

(1) 선행사가 사람과 동물일 때

A man and his dog **that** were passing by were injured.

(2) 최상급, 서수사, the very, the only, the same, every, all 다음에서

He is the greatest poet **that** Korea has ever produced.

(3) 의문 대명사 who, what, which 다음에서

Who **that** has common sense can believe such an thing?

4. What의 용법

My teacher made me **what** I am now.

I really mean **what** I say.(선행사 포함 관계대명사)

He is clever, and **what** is better still, very brave.

What was worse, all the product's nightmares came true.

↳ 뒷 문장 전체, 앞부분은 선행사절

<what의 관용적 표현>

- A is to B what(=as) C is to D : A가 B에 대한 관계는 C가 D에 대한 관계와 같다.

  Leaves **are to** the plant **what** lungs **are to** the animal.

- what with(by) A and what with(by) B : 한편으로는 A하고, 또 한편으로는 B 해서~.

  What with overwork and (**what with**) undernourishment, he fell ill.

- What I am - 현재의 나

  What I was - 과거의 나

  What I have - 현재의 나의 재산

  He made me what I am.

- what we(you, they) call, what is called : 소위, 이른바, 말하자면

  (=so to speak, as it were)

  He is, **what we call,** a self-made man.

- what is more : 게다가

  what is better : 더욱 더 좋은 것은 , 금상첨화로

  what is worse : 더욱 더 나쁜 것은, 설상가상으로

  what is more important : 더 중요한 것은

  The book is interesting and, **what** is **more** important, very instructive.

B. 관계대명사의 생략

(1) 타동사 또는 전치사의 목적격으로 쓰일 때

This is the boy (**whom**) we met yesterday.

(2) 관계대명사가 주격 보어 또는 목적격 보어로 쓰일 때

He is not the man (**which** 또는 **that**) he was two years ago.

(3) 관계대명사 다음에 there is, there are가 계속될 때

He taught me the difference (**that**) **there** is between right and wrong.

(4) there is, here is, it is, what is, who is로 시작하는 구문에서

There is a boy (who) wants to see you.

C. 의사 관계대명사 : As, Than, But (주격, 목적격이 있다)

(1) 선행사가 as, such, the same이 있을 때 as를 사용

- As many men as came were caught.
- Such books as you have given me are worthless.
- You are just the same as you always were.

(2) 부정 어구가 붙은 선행사 뒤에 but을 쓴다.(=that~not)

but 자체도 부정의 의미가 있으므로 이중 부정(→강한긍정)의 문장을 만든다.

- There is **no** one **but** knows the novelist.

(3) 비교급이 붙는 선행사 뒤에 쓰이는 than(~보다의 뜻)

- Things went better **than** had been expected.

D. 복합 관계대명사 : 관계대명사 + ever

(1) 명사절(선행사+관계대명사 역할)

- **Anyone** can come. **He** wishes to come.

→ **Anyone who wishes to come** can come.(형용사절)

→ **Whoever wishes to come** can come.(명사절)

(2) 양보 부사절(may사용)

- Whoever may break this law, he will be punished. (whoever=no matter who)

(3) 형용사 용법 : 복합관계대명사 명사 수식하는 경우, whosever는 없음.

- Take whichever book you like.(=any book that)

E. 관계형용사 : 관계대명사 +명사

- You may take **which book** you like.
- The letter was written in French, **which language** he could not understand.
- I gave him **what money** (= all the money that) I had.
- He has sold **what few books** (= all the few books that) he had.

II. Sentence Structure

1. More teachers _____ are qualified to teach French subjects in French are still needed.
   (A) whom (B) who
   (C) which (D) whose

2. The World Cup, _____ is the most watched sporting event in the world, is held every four years.
   (A) who (B) which
   (C) whose (D) that

3. Mr. Anderson is the man _____ I met at the motor show last year in Busan.
   (A) which (B) whose
   (C) whom (D) what

4. The Monet Foundation is an organization _____ mission is to support public art projects.
   (A) that (B) which
   (C) whom (D) whose

5. The person who _____ the best sales plan will be awarded a 500 dollar bonus.
   (A) creating (B) is created
   (C) have created (D) creates

6. They provided us with coupons _____ can be used at hotels and stores.
   (A) whichever (B) whatever
   (C) which (D) what

7. A lot of people _____ invested in the fund believed that they will gain a large profit.
   (A) which (B) what
   (C) whose (D) that

연구 및 정답

1. (B) 선행사(사람) + 주격관계사 + 동사.
2. (B) 앞에 부분을 받는 관계사 which(and it).
3. (C) 목적격 관계사.
4. (D) 소유격 관계사 + 명사.
5. (D) 선행명사 + 주격관계사 + 동사(선행명사와 수 일치).
6. (C) 선행사 사물인 주격관계사(which, that) + 동사.
7. (D) 선행사 사람인 주격관계사(who, that)가 정답.

1. He was attending the meeting _____ was held at the BEST Convention Center in Tokyo.
   (A) that (B) of which
   (C) who (D) whom

2. The trainer, _____ lecturing experience spans more than ten years, is famous for his interesting speeches.
   (A) whose (B) whom
   (C) who (D) which

3. The shipment of the items _____ you ordered from our shoe store will be delayed because of bad weather.
   (A) what (B) which
   (C) who (D) who

4. Interviewees need to figure out _____ interviewers consider important.
   (A) what (B) which
   (C) who (D) that

5. Maple Park, _____ is popular with tourists, will be renovated next year.
   (A) which (B) what
   (C) whom (D) that

6. _____ laugh last laugh longest.
   (A) He who (B) He whom
   (C) Those who (D) Those whom

7. Linda is the student _____ I think is the best in the school.
   (A) who (B) whom
   (C) whose (D) which

연구 및 정답

1. (A) 선행사 주격관계사(사물) which, that이 정답.
2. (A) 선행사 사람 소유격 관계사.
3. (B) 선행사 사물 목적격 관계사.
4. (A) 선행사를 포함하는 관계대명사 what.
5. (A) 앞의 선행사를 받는 관계대명사는?
6. (C) Those who + V 주격 관계대명사, -하는 사람들.
7. (A) the student who (I think) is.

1. It is the first step _____ the most difficult.
   (A) who is (B) which are
   (C) that is (D) that are

2. I want to give you _____ you need.
   (A) that (B) what
   (C) the thing what (D) which

3. They always give the best seat to ______ comes first.
   (A) which (B) whom
   (C) whomever (D) whoever

4. I have three best friends, one of _____ is a famous film director.
   (A) who (B) whom
   (C) that (D) them

5. The Good Earth, ______, is a novel about China.
   (A) was written by Pearl Buck (B) which written by Pearl Buck
   (C) which was written by Pearl Buck (D) that was written by Pearl Buck

6. The tree, _____ are almost bare now, is more than three hundred years old.
   (A) the whose branches (B) the branches of which
   (C) of which branches (D) the branches of whose

7. She is one of the few girls who _____ passed the examination.
   (A) has (B) have
   (C) had (D) was

연구 및 정답

1. (C) 주격 관계대명사 선행사와 수 일치시켜야 함.
2. (B) 선행사 포함 관계대명사.
3. (D) anyone who comes first(whoever comes first).
4. (B) 전치사 + 목적격 관계대명사(사람).
5. (C) which was written by.
6. (B) the 명사 of which(whose 명사).
7. (B) one of the 복수명사 who 복수동사.

Ⅲ. Grammar Practice

1. Private radio stations in the United States are supported by the money received from
A B
advertisers whose buy time to broadcast sales messages.
C D

2. Heart Like a Wheel is the movie biography of Shirley Muldowney, a waitress from
A B
New York, whom became a successful hot rod driver.
C D

3. The adder is a snake has a relatively stout body, a short tail, and a flat head.
A B C D

4. Aara Mayo, a physician and surgeon, helped establish the New Orleans hospital who
A B C
became her name.
D

5. Tenant farmers are those they either rent a farm and work it for themselves or work the
A B C
farm for the owner and receive payment.
D

6. People which live in a metropolitan area often have little feeling of political unity among
A B C D
themselves.

7. Vegetable oil is an oil that come from seeds, flowers, or fruits.
A B C D

연구 및 정답

1. (C) 동사 buy로 보아 주격 관계대명사가 와야 한다. whose → who.
2. (C) whom → who.
3. (A) snake와 has를 연결하는 관계대명사가 필요하다.
4. (C) 선행사가 사물이므로 who를 which 혹은 that으로 고쳐야 한다.
5. (A) 선행사가 사람을 나타내는 주격이기 때문에 관계대명사도 주격이어야 한다.
   they → who.
6. (A) 선행사가 사람이다. which → who.
7. (B) 관계대명사의 선행사 an oil이 단수임에 착안할 것.

1. The term "social interaction" refers particularly (A) to contact (B) between (C) persons what (D) depend on each other.

2. Edward Albee's early plays are marked by themes associated with the theater of the absurd, in whom (A) characters suffer (B) from an inability (C) to communicate meaningfully (D).

3. Mrs. Swanson, a member of the social committee for the coming (A) year, is (B) the only (C) woman which (D) has a car.

4. At the turn (A) of the century, any girl which (B) had a college education was automatically considered (C) to be bright (D).

5. Jerboas are long-eared (A) rodents that they (B) look like (C) tiny (D) kangaroos.

6. Although (A) I expected something different (B), I was still surprised (C) by which (D) he said.

7. Most people (A) know that (B) it is like to have (C) their blood pressure taken, but few understand the meaning of the numbers used to record (D) blood pressure.

연구 및 정답

1. (D) 관계대명사의 선행사가 persons이므로 D를 who로 고친다.
2. (A) 관계대명사의 선행사가 the theater of the absurd이다. whom → which.
3. (D) 선행사는 woman, 그 앞의 the only가 hint.
4. (B) 선행사 girl이 any로 제한되므로 that, who도 가능.
5. (B) B는 선행사 rodents를 받는 관계대명사이며, look의 주절이므로 they는 불필요.
6. (D) D에는 said의 목적어임과 동시에 선행사까지 포함된 관계대명사인 what이 요구됨. by의 목적어는 what he said임.
7. (B) B는 "what is it like to have...?"

Ⅳ. Vocabulary

※ Choose the one which has the closest meaning with the underlined part.

1. The chukchi of the Siberian Arctic bred reindeer as a source of food.
   (A) trapped (B) raised
   (C) chased (D) tamed
2. Jack is defrauding the commercial law.
   (A) discarding (B) maiming
   (C) cheating (D) repealing
3. These scissors are blunt and can not cut paper.
   (A) weak (B) small
   (C) broken (D) dull
4. I saw the balls wobble on the table and the roll off.
   (A) shake (B) teeter
   (C) float (D) vanish
5. Excessive humidity, retards evaporation of perspiration from the body.
   (A) prevents (B) slows
   (C) disturbs (D) restraints
6. Mechanics is the study of the effect of forces on the bodies or liquids at rest or in motion.
   (A) atoms (B) objects
   (C) gasses (D) fluids
7. These instructions are mandatory; any violation will be severely punished.
   (A) obligatory (B) willing
   (C) voluntary (D) effective
8. To the Sioux, the symbol of a cross represented a dragonfly with its wings outstretched.
   (A) rising (B) spread
   (C) torn (D) missing

연구

1. breed: raise, keep. trap 올가미를 놓다.
2. defrauding 횡령하는, 사취하는. discarding 버리는, 폐기하는. repeal 무효로 하다.
3. blunt: 둔한.
4. wobble 흔들리다(= teeter).
5. evaporation 증발, 탈수. disturb: stir up. restrain: hold back, check.
6. atom 원자. fluid: liquid.
7. mandatory: 의무적인. voluntary 자발적인.
8. outstretched 펼친, 뻗친.

정답

1. B 2. C 3. D 4. B 5. B 6. D 7. A 8. B

1. Conversely, in their judical role the agencies should act more like court.
   (A) Directly (B) Narrowly
   (C) Reversely (D) Pointedly

2. Each agency's attention to one segment of the economy would develop an expertise essential to wise regulation.
   (A) experiment (B) expense
   (C) expertness (D) enterprise

3. The night was so foggy that the murderer was easily able to escape his pursuers.
   (A) misty (B) cold
   (C) hot (D) messy

4. In recent years many cities have made significant cutbacks in the provision of municipal services.
   (A) reductions (B) payoffs
   (C) improvements (D) breakdown

5. Negotiations between the port employers and unions again ended in the deadlock.
   (A) standstill (B) success
   (C) agreement (D) danger

6. There was a glut of spare parts that had to be stockpiled in the storage room.
   (A) excess (B) gourmet
   (C) hasten (D) retard

7. Fidelity is quality of character that is admired by most people.
   (A) faithfulness (B) generosity
   (C) chastity (D) wisdom

연구

1. conversely 거꾸로, 반대의.
2. expertise 전문가적 의견(기술). enterprise: project, plan.
3. foggy 안개가 자욱한
4. cutback 감소
5. deadlock 막다른 상태, 교착 상태. standstill: stop, halt.
6. glut 초과, 과다(excess)
7. fidelity 신의, 충실함

정답

1. C 2. C 3. A 4. A 5. A 6. A 7. A

부 록

Part (A) Sentence Constituent

1. Byron (They, The student in the class) listened to the song.

2. Jessica (is, has been, might have been) busy with her work.

3. Geoff understands (the answer, them, that she can't come.)

4.

Ms. Tracy	gave	us	assignments.
They	will send	their grandmother	postcards.
A staff member	found	them	a room.
The teacher	is telling	the students	an interesting story.

5. Lynda is (my sister, charming.)
   It seems (quite unbelievable to us, that she lied.)

6.

They	elected	him	their new president.
The heater	will keep	the room	warm.
The photograph	makes	him	look younger.

7. My uncle	smokes	very heavily.
He	didn't study	when he was young.
Cheryl	is	at college.
He	put the files	in the drawer.

Part (B) English Structure

A. The Principles of English Structure

a) The End Focus Principle

b) The End Weight Principle

c) The Bolinger Principle

d) The Proximity Principle

e) The Nonintervention Principle

f) The Modification Principle

g) The Iconicity Principle

h) The Neighborhood Principle

B. Basic English Sentences

1. I made for the door.
2. He will make a good doctor.
3. He made the box yesterday.
4. He made her a doll.
5. He made her happy.

C. English Clauses

1. It is true **that he bought a house.**

   The truth is **that they cheated on the exam.**

   I am glad **that you enjoyed the meal.**

   He told us **you would find out the result.**

   The fact that he is poor is known to everybody.

   The question is **whether they would be satisfied.**

   I don't know **when they will arrive here.**

2. Barbara works for a company **that makes washing machines.**

   These are principles **which we all have to follow.**

3. She wears headphones **as she studies.**

   You can't camp **where you like in this area.**

   Because my rent was overdue, the landlord evicted me.

   He said he would join the club **if you do too.**

   Though I'd like to help, your husband will be jealous for me.

   While I am willing to help you, I don't have much time.

Part (C) : Structure Review

1. Frances Perkins **became** the first female member of a United States cabinet.

   Portraiture **became** almost a fad in the 1780's and 1790's.

   Albert Gore, Jr **became** the forty-fifth Vice president of the United States.

   John won't (***become, make, be**) a good doctor.

2. She **was named** secretary of labor in 1933.

   Chaucer **is called** the Father of English poetry.

   He **was appointed** head of the meeting.

3. Their feathers are stiffer and smoother than **those** of most other birds.

   The lenses in an optical microscope bend the light passing through a specimen to form an image of that specimen **that is much larger than the one actually viewed.**

   When lava reached the surface, its temperature can be ten times **that** of boiling water.

   Characters in realistic literature tend to be more complex than **those** in romantic literature.

   The houses of the rich are much larger than **those** of the poor.

   Expected noises are usually more tolerable than **unexpected ones** of the same magnitude.

   Our exported goods are recognized all over the world and are superior to **those** of rival firms.

   The nutritional benefits of vitamin supplements are far less than **those** of natural food sources.

   Jerry Hallmark's vast experience in overseas sales, and **that** of his secretary's made the pair the obvious choice to head the new branch office in Paris.

4. The artist's main function is to describe as accurately and honestly as possible **what is observed through the senses.**

It happened **that I was out of London at that time.**

Entered **the man who was soft in appearance but hard in reality.**

What we accept rationally we often find it hard to put into practice.

How great a sacrifice it was, no one but him would ever know.

Descriptive statistics is a tool for describing, or summarizing or reducing to comprehensible form **the properties of an otherwise unwieldy mass of data.**

5. I have known him **to lose** his temper very often.('to' is deleted in British English)

   I have never known a man **to die** of love.

6. His views are alarming his audience.

   * His views are **very** alarming his audience.

   He was annoyed by the policeman.

   * He was **very** annoyed by the policeman.

   He was **very** disturbed by her attitude.

7. **Located** in lower Manhattan in New York City, the World Trade Center was completed in 1973 at a cost of $750 million.

   Erected at the turn of the century, the Minnesota State Capitol building is made of white granite and marble.

   First designated in 1970, Earth Day has become an annual international event **dedicated to raising** concerns about environmental issues such as pollution.

   Declared an endangered species in the United States, the ginseng root has been gathered almost to the point of extinction.

   Found in all parts of the state, pines are the most common tree in Georgia.

   Heavily built, with poor vision but excellent senses of smell and hearing, the bear will eat almost anything.

8. **Although mainly eaten** for their flavor, mushrooms are of some nutritional value.

   When well fitted, glasses can correct most sight defects in healthy eyes.

When seen through a telescope, Venus appears to go through changes in size and shape.

People who reverse the letters of words **when trying to read** suffer from dyslexia.

When building nests during spring nesting season, Canadian geese are fiercely territorial.

Until recently proven incorrect, astronomers had assumed that the insides of whitedwarfs were uniform.

Although well intended, early approaches for coping with workplace stress dealt with the problem only after its symptoms had appeared.

If freshly squeezed, the orange juice in a one-cup serving provides twice the minimum daily requirement for vitamin C.

When overcome by excitement, people may have trouble thinking clearly.

Children, she believes, are supposed to answer politely **when spoken to by an adult.**

No one under the age of seven will be admitted to the concert **unless accompanied by an adult.**

Unless authorized by the security officer, you may not enter the building after working hours.

Once consolidated, the two divisions will perform their tasks better and, therefore, attract more customers.

Anyone without an invitation will not be allowed to attend the show, **unless accompanied by a membership cardholder.**

9. Only warm and extremely moist air can supply the energy **necessary** to spawn and maintain tropical storms.

   Cadmium is a chemical **useful** in the manufacture of artists' pigments, automobile enamels, vinyl plastics, in addition to phosphors for color television tubes.

10. The first commercial film **made** in California was completed in 1932.

    The university of Georgia, **chartered** in 1785, was the first state-supported university in the United States.

    Ann Beattie's collection comprises three dozen stories **written** over a 25-year period.

    Emma Lazarus wrote the sonnet **inscribed** on the pedestal of the Statue of Liberty.

Rubber **produced** from vulcanized silicons with a high molecular weight is difficult to distinguish from natural rubber.

The musical instrument **called** the basis is six feet long.

The smallest snails and clams are often carried from place to place **embedded** in the mud on the feet of wading birds.

In the judicial system of the United States, defendants **found** not guilty of the charges of which they are tried are automatically acquitted.

The microscope evolved slowly, its development **hampered** by the lack of both theoretical understanding or necessarily mechanical technology.

We are going to talk about the problem **discussed** at the last meeting.

I'd like the **collected** works of Maugham.

I have written about the changes in the social system **required** to promote happiness.

We can supplement our own ideas with information and data **gathered** from our reading.

According to corporate rules, exaggerated or false information **given** on personal background surveys can lead to dismissal.

The information **provided by him** was not relevant to the case.

Inside Science is a magazine **published** monthly by the National Association of Scientists.

11. Neon is said to be inert **because** it does not react easily with other substances.

A bank official contacted me **because** she discovered that a suspicious transaction had occurred in my account.

Nearly every aspect of economic life is affected **by** seasonal variations.

Most living creatures depend on plants **for** their nourishment.

The number of people purchasing homes is still on the rise **despite** a significant increase in mortgage rates.

Kokanee salmon begin to deteriorate and die soon **after spawning** at the age of four.

After several unsuccessful attempts, Robert Peary reached the North Pole on April 6, 1909.

Because of his reservations about the issue, the senator refused to vote for it.

During his life, Eugene O'Neill was regarded as the foremost American dramatist.

Copper tubing is the preferred choice of plumbers **since it is noncorrosive.**

12. Ball-point pens require a thicker ink **than fountain pens do.**

Ball-point pens require a thicker ink **than fountain pens.**

Ball-point pens require a thicker ink **than do fountain pens.**

Jane is taller than John.

Jane is taller than John is.

He is a man more clever than Mary.

* He is a more clever man than Mary.

She is a taller woman than Mary.

She is a woman taller than Mary.

There is no man richer in the town than he is.

* There is no richer man in the town than he is.

Overexposure to the sun can produce more damage to the skin **than can some toxic chemicals.**

Liberals tend to favor more immediate social change **than do conservatives.**

Microscopes make small things appear larger **than they really are.**

In bas-relief sculpture, a design projects very slightly from its background, **as on some coins.**

13. The city of Montreal **covers over 70 square miles.**

Scholars **have counted about 3,000 spoken languages.**

14. Author Edith Wharton thoroughly understood **the society in which she had grown up.**

Many birds have feathers **whose** colors blend with their surroundings.

Mosaic is the art of closely setting small things into a surface **to create a decorative design.**

(* that a decorative design is created)

Janet Collins' struggle to make a place for herself in ballet is the kind of life story **about which a fascinating novel might be written.**

Toward the end of his life, John Singer Sargent returned to the painting of landscapes and the use of watercolors, **in which he excelled.**

He is the man **who I think is honest.**

He is the man **whom I think to be honest.**

Through microscopes people can see objects **that are invisible to the naked eye.**

The boy **whom I believed to be honest** deceived me.

I will employ the man **who they say is a fluent speaker of English.**

One **whose desires and impulses are not his own** has no character.

There are many organizations **whose** sole purpose is to help mentally retarded children.

Although humans age, **the rate at which this process occurs** is different with each person.

A boy **whom** you must meet right away is Freddy Thompson, the best math student in our dormitory.

Any student whose master's thesis is not submitted a month prior to graduation will not fulfill the graduation requirements.

The columnist feels sure that **whoever** wins the election will have the support of both parties.

That rich woman offered a reward to whoever should restore her lost car.

In an effort to educate potential clients on our new line of products, we offer a product brochure **to whoever visits our store.**

Whichever team wins the game will receive a cash award of $100,000 and have a chance to participate in the upcoming world competition.

After tonight, he would never be **the same man** as he was before.

Sam had a **louder voice than** the other speakers, but unfortunately the louder his voice became, the less attention he got.

There is no work whatever **but he can criticize.**

Some newcomers may experience difficulty using administrative forms **that they have never seen before.**

They left on Monday, **since when** we have heard nothing.

15. A logarithm is **what is known in algebra as an exponent.**

That(*What) he is honest is true.

What(*That) I want is a book.

Most people know **what it is like** to have their blood pressure taken, but few understand the meaning of the numbers used to record blood pressure.

I know **that** snow is like down.

Many people are unaware that prairies once existed **in what is now the state of Michigan.**

The first British attempt to establish a colony **in what is now the United States** took place in 1585.

What is most touching in O. Henry's stories is the gallantry with which ordinary people struggle to maintain their dignity.

What ranks as the most important crop in Hawaii is sugar cane.

What appears in the first draft of the budget will not necessarily be in the final draft.

That it took our experts a whole week to complete the simple calculations is incomprehensible to us.

To stay competitive, we must understand **what other industry leaders are striving to achieve.**

16. Nearly one-fifth **the size of** the continental United States, Alaska is the largest state in the Union.

He must have **something the matter** with his feet.

17. Hudson Bay area is snowbound for **most of the year.**

Most of the people are afraid of snakes.

Many of the physical characteristics that distinguish human beings from other primates are related to the ability of people to stand upright and walk on two legs.

18. **The first woman appointed by a United States President to a cabinet position,** Frances Perkins held the post of labor secretary for twelve years.

Mercury, the only metal that is liquid at ordinary temperature, is the heaviest liquid known.

Martha Graham, one of the great modern choreographers, has run her own dance company for a half century.

Patty Berg, the top tournament winner in women's golf won eight-three golf tournaments from 1935 through 1964.

William Pitt Fessenden, a United States senator from Maine, helped found the Republican party in the 1850's.

19. A stream of volcanic lava flows differently, **depending on** the sort of ground it flows over.

With age, the mineral content of human bones decreases, **thereby making** them more fragile.

The face of the Moon is changed by collisions with meteoroids, **causing** new craters to appear.

Elizabeth Bishop's poems are frequently long and carefully constructed, **using elaborate rhyme or half-rhymes.**

High technology venture firms keep growing in size, **hiring** numerous college graduates with degrees in engineering and technology.

20. **There are** large amounts of vitamin E in green leaves, such as lettuce, and in cereals.

In the United States there are approximately four million miles of roads, street, and highways.

There are many different kinds of maps.

There **is** a book and two pencils on the table.(informal)

21. **Not only is rice eaten as a cooked dish the world over,** but it is also used as the base of many other food, condiments, and even beverages.

Not until the eighteenth century did scientists begin to appreciate the complex chemistry of metallurgy.

Not until Kentucky's Mammoth Cave had been completely explored in 1972 was its full extent realized.

Only in the past decade have meteorologists begun to understand that the air and the oceans act as a single fluid when they exchange heat and gases.

Nowhere are retail trade figures more skewed than in the auto industry.

Rarely are observations located near city lights or at lower elevations.

Only for a short period of time do cheetahs run at top speed.

Little did I dream that she would pass the exam.

Rarely do meteors blaze for more than a few seconds once they enter the Earth's atmosphere.

Not until the 1960's, did Theodore Mainman at Hudson Research laboratories build the world's first working laser.

Under no circumstances, must the door be left unlocked.

Only in this way is it possible to explain their actions.

In no other way can the matter be explained.

Not even there did it rain.

By no properly qualified technician has this instrument ever been adequately tested.

On no account are visitors allowed to feed the animals.

Only after she had been served with the subpoena did Mrs. Arbor turn over the confidential report to Mr. Harris, the head of the commission, and me, its treasurer.

Not only may such a love have deepened and exalted, but may still deepen and exalt, the life of any man of any age.

22. **Scattered** across the United States **are** more than 1,200 art museums.

Contained on the 23 pairs of chromosomes in the nucleus of the human cell **is** the complex set of instructions known as the human genome.

Featured at the Henry Ford Museum **is** an exhibit of antique cars dating from 1865.

Located behind each eyelid **are** the two lacrimal glands.

Especially important to many people **is** legislation against pollution.

Characteristic of Op Art **are** the carefully arranged hues and geometric patterns that create optical illusions.

More important has been the establishment of legal services.

Equally difficult would be a solution to Russell's paradox.

Her face was stony and **even stonier was** the tone of her voice.

Of particular relevance are such results as inversion, emphasis and agreement.

Sitting at her desk in deep concentration **was** my sister.

Addressing the demonstration **was** a quite elderly woman.

23. Some mammals migrate to warmer areas **when winter comes.**

When he comes, I will leave.

I know **when he will leave.**

We will ship your order **as soon as you send** us a written confirmation.

After you have completed filling in the form, we will discuss the possibility of hiring you.

With the new processing unit, buyers can check their orders for errors **before they submit.**

If it rains tomorrow, I won't go out.

24. Anesthetics **are used to** cause insensitivity to pain during surgical operation.

I **am used to getting** up early.

I **used to** visit the beautiful lake.

The gray scale, a progressive series of shades ranging from black to white, **is used** in computer graphics **to add detail** to graphical images.

25. **That the dog was the first animal to be domesticated** is generally agreed upon by authorities in the field.

That the Moon appears considerably larger at the horizon than it does overhead is merely an optical illusion.

That cultural anthropology has not attained a state of complete coherence is true.

26. Anthropology is a science **in that anthropologists use** a rigorous set of methods and techniques to document observations that can be checked by others.

The commutation of a criminal's sentence differs from a pardon **in that it reduces** the terms of punishment rather than excuses the criminal completely.

Advertising is distinguished from other forms of communication **in that the advertiser pays for the message to be delivered.**

My grandpa was a decent person **except that he was rather lazy.**

The play went well, **except that a few people forgot their lines.**

27. A tariff is customarily collected on goods **coming** into a country.

Experiments **using gene therapy** represent a giant step into the medicine of the future.

Air **containing the carbon dioxide** necessary for photosynthesis enters leaves through tiny surface openings.

The slide rule uses sliding scales with marks **representing numbers and their logarithms.**

The average age of the Mediterranean olive trees **growing today is two hundred years.**

Most international flights **serving** in-flight meals usually offer chicken or beef dishes, since those two meals are the most preferred by travelers all over the world.

People **working** in the warehouse after hours are advised to stay inside the building and keep the doors locked.

28. Hawks serve an important purpose in the scheme of nature **by preying on** destructive rodents, such as mice and rats.

By adopting laws excluding competition from an industry, governments have often created public service monopolies.

Bats avoid running into objects **by emitting** high-frequency sounds and listening for echoes.

29. Computers that once took up entire rooms are now **small enough** to put on desktops and into wristwatches.

30. The goal of teaching is to help students learn **what they need to know to live** a well-adjusted and successful life.

One purpose of value theory in economics is to explain **how the prices of goods and services are determined.**

The various types of bacteria are classified according to **how they are shaped.**

Scientists are now beginning to conduct experiments on **how noise pollution can trigger different sorts of health risks.**

There are geographic, economic, and cultural reasons **why diets differ around the world.**

Chemists are not sure precisely **how cold fusion can occur.**

Do you know **what time the movie starts?**

Those who were left alone in the cave know better than the others **what frightening sounds bats flying about in the dark make.**

31. The sapphire's transparency to ultraviolet and infrared radiation **makes it useful** in optical instrument.

The powerful jaws and sharp teeth of the piranha **make it a dangerous and feared fish.**

The development of steam engines, gasoline engines, and electric motors in the early 1800's **made it possible to replace hand tools** with machine tools.

In art, the tendency of gouache colors to lighten on drying **makes possible** a wide range of pearly or pastel-like effects.

Spectrographs **make it possible for phoneticians to analyze the human voice and its speech qualities.**

Machines have made **possible the mass production of all kinds of goods.**

X-rays are to pass through objects and thus **make visible details that are otherwise impossible to observe.**

The use of radar as well as the two-way radio **makes it possible for the police to intercept most speeders.**

The computer **makes possible a phenomenal leap in human proficiency.**

He has made it clear that he is not going to change his mind.

32. **The skeleton of an insect** is on the outside of its body.

 The background and early life of Mary should be reviewed here.

33. Charles Schulz's comic strip "Peanuts," features children who make **funny but wise** statements.

 It was a **boring if instructive** lecture.

 It was an **instructive but boring** lecture.

 Such a decision will bring about **harmful if not fatal** results.

 More than twelve hours of my school week are spent in one of **the dingiest yet versatile** rooms of the building.

 Optical painting overlaps with **some, though not all,** aspects of color-field painting.

34. **Like likes like.**

 But me no buts.

 Mothers **mother** their children.

 Food seasoning plays an important role in the cooking customs of many cultures in the world.

 The use of small airlines enables potato farmers to **dust** their crops.

 She **fasted** her illness off.

 John **doctored** the horses with a strong-smelling ointment.

 His car **was totaled** in the accident.

35. For the advertiser, one of the greatest appeals of radio is **that it has an audience all day long.**

 One problem with all languages is **that they are full of irregularities**

36. Of the 300 languages that were once spoken by Native American people, **an estimated 150 languages** exist today.

 a startling 65,000 tons of valuable cargo

 a hundred books

37. It is prohibited by law to mail through parcel post any merchandise that **might prove dangerous** in transport.

    I like the Mozart's music very much because his music **sounds sweet and soothing.**

    It seemed to Mr.s Garber that the butter **smelled somewhat bad.**

    The situation there **looked so serious.**

    He was determined to eat it all, even though it **tasted bitter** to him.

    However, since no ammonia fumes are detected, this theory does not **seem credible.**

    I never **feel bad** if after trying hard I fail to win a prize.

    Also by radio waves you may fry eggs on a stove that never **gets hot** enough to burn paper or burn you if you should touch it.

38. California has **more** land under irrigation **than any other state.**

    Many jazz enthusiasts rate Charlie "Bird" Parker, the alto saxophonists, **as the greatest** improviser of all jazz musicians.

39. **Among the most important jazz innovators in the twentieth century** are Louis Armstrong, Fletcher Henderson, Duke Ellington, and Dizzy Gillespie.

    Out of John Kenneth Galbraith's The Affluent Society came the argument for an increase in public goods, potentially at the expense of private goods.

    In the Morgan Library in New York City is a collection of medieval and Renaissance manuscripts.

    Among the most revealing aspects of mining towns was their paucity of public open space.

    In the northern and central parts of the state of Idaho are found majestic mountains and churning rivers.

    Southwest of Omaha, Nebraska, lies Lincoln, the state's educational and governmental center.

40. **The closer** to one of the Earth's poles, **the greater** the gravitational force.

    The more he has, **the more** he wants.

The stronger the magnet, **the greater** the number of lines of magnetic force.

Of the two houses the family prefers **the more isolated one.**

I've worked for two companies, Darlingtons and Kenworth, and of the two, Darlingtons offers **the more comprehensive** benefits.

The coarser the sediment, **the steeper and narrower** the beach.

The more we attempted to explain our mistake, **the worse** our story sounded.

The quicker a loan is repaid, **the less** it will cost.

The longer you own your house, the less transfer taxes will be imposed on the property when you sell it.

According to an article published in Forbes magazine, **the larger** a company is, **the less** satisfied the employees who work for it are.

41. **It** is the recommendation of the U.S. Public Health Service **that** all children be vaccinated against a variety of diseases.

It is impossible to define a clear upper boundary of the atmosphere.

Someone remarks on what a lucky coincidence **it is that Earth is perfectly suited for life.**

42. Under the educational plan proposed by the school board of Rocklyn County, **were parents unhappy** with a particular school, they **could simply move** their children to another.

According to the World Health Organization, **were any of the six most dangerous diseases to break out**, it could be cause for quarantine.

Were the Office of Management inclined to push for such a reduction, it would probably not be successful.

The impact of Thoreau's "On the Duty of Civil Disobedience" might not have been so far-reaching **had it not been for Elizabeth Peabody**, who dared to publish the controversial essay.

43. The economic background of labor legislation will not be mentioned in this course, **nor will trade unionism.**

Your criticism of the three short stories should not be less 2,000 words, **nor should it be more than 3,000.**

Those who favor the new law say that the present law does not set spending limits on lobbyists' gifts to politicians, **nor does it limit statewide funds.**

A sneeze cannot be performed voluntarily, **nor can it be easily suppressed.**

The brown thrasher is not a particularly large or strong bird, **nor is it equipped for fighting.**

44. **The problem has already been discussed by the board of directors** when it was proposed again by the supervisors.

Much of the carnage of elephants, giraffes, and big cats **must have been committed by uncaring hunters.**

The X-Ray treatments were given daily up to the time that he was dismissed from the hospital.

The Military Academy at West Point **is located on** the west bank of the Hudson River, north of north of New York City.

Presidential elections are held every four years on the first Tuesday after the firs Monday in November.

Are all telephone numbers **listed** in the directory?

What holidays **are celebrated in** your country?

English **is spoken** all over the world.

Bees **are exposed to** many hardships and many dangers.

45. Researchers have long debated **whether Saturn's moon Titan contains hydrocarbon oceans and lakes.**

Why some satellites have retrograde motion is not yet understood.

When and by whom the islands of the West Indies were first settled is a matter of debate among archaeologists.

When zero was first invented is not known.

I can't imagine **what they want with your address.**

The problem depends (on) **who will water my plants.**

When numbers were created is not known.

There has been a debate **(as to) which theory is the better.**

I had many struggles with myself **(as to) what course of life I should take.**

He is thankful **(for) what I have done for him.**

46. **Does he have a hard time speaking** English?

We had a very hard time discussing some of the problems.

We had difficulty finding the obscure path through the forest.

Did you have any trouble driving through the snow?

Most of them have spent their time in playing baseball.

She was busy preparing for her trip to Brazil and Chile.

A bat will often **spend** the daylight hours **hanging** upside down in a tree or cave.

Marmots **spend** their time foraging among meadow plants and flowers or **sunning** on rocky cliffs.

47. Copper is the favored metal for electricians' wire **because of its excellent conductivity.**

(* excellent conductivity of it)

The Growth of the City(*The Growth of it)(Its growth)

Regardless of its location(*the location of it) or facilities, a park is intended for the enjoyment of all.

48. He gave me several reasons, **only a few of which (*them) were valid.**

I picked up the apples, **some of which were badly bruised.**

A number of suggestions were made at the meeting, **most of which were not practical.**

As a start-up venture company, we have only three branches nationwide and a total of 25 employees, **most of whom are graphic designers.**

49. He gave me **a (the) book** which he bought yesterday.

Astronomy is **the science** of stars and plants.

50. She gave him a book.(preferable)

She gave a book to him.

* John gave Mary it.

A book is on the table.

There is a book on the table.(preferable)

* There is the book on the table.

51. This book sells well.

This novel reads easily.

52. He could pronounce each word distinctly.

* He could pronounce distinctly each word.

cf) He looked at me suspiciously. (He looked suspiciously at me.)

However hard he may study, he will fail in the test.

However carefully you drive, you will probably have an accident eventually.

I wonder how soon he will come.

However cold it is, she always goes swimming.

The longer he stayed, the more sullen he became.

No matter how dry a desert may be, it is not necessarily worthless.

I was surprised how easy it was to use the computer.

53. In no clothes Miss Kim looks attractive.

In no clothes does Miss Kim look attractive.

Not even ten years ago we could see such a film.

Not even ten years ago could we see such a film.

Across the street is a store.

Across the street there is a store.

He found parking difficult.(general)

He found it difficult to park.(temporary)

Tom comes here.(habitual)

Here comes Tom. (now)

We live near the sea.(Perhaps five kilometers away)

We live by the sea. (We can see it)

54. He is a friend of mine.

He is my friend.

55. **Acquiring education** is the principal way of gaining status in a culture that generally stresses achievement, skillfulness, and upward mobility.

Collecting dolls as a hobby becomes increasingly popular during the past fifty years.

His working all night in the rain caused him to catch a cold.

Exercising daily promotes physical as well as emotional well-being in people of all ages.

Separating all of these materials and recovering them for reuse can be very expensive.

Preference should be given to those whose applications are received by next Tuesday.

Developing successful programs to increase parents' participation in school activities is the main objective of our organization.

56. **(To overcome)(*For overcoming) the stiffness of his legs,** Jones regularly took long hikes on Mount Adams, the great peak of the Cascades.

(To settle the problems)(*For settling the problems), we must take a giant step.

a device **for settling the problem**

To earn(*For earning) the accounting certificate, I had to attend four, two-hour classes a day for a month and review what I learned in school each day until after midnight every night.

For completing(*To complete) the course given by the Federal Certification Board, each trainee will receive an accounting certificate as a symbol of competence.

57. He changed.

He was changed.

He appeared.

* He was appeared.

He turned the pages.(The pages were turned by him.)

He turned the corner.(*The corner was turned by him.)

An accident occurred(*was occurred) last night.

58. If my explanation **is confusing** to you, you **get confused** when you hear it.

Lead has been used as a material for sculpture since the time of the early Greek.

Milk proteins are valued for their high nutritional content.

Volcanoes are described as active, dormant, or extinct.

Nonmetallic minerals are found in various places around the world.

Modern dance is taught in the same kinds of studios as ballet.

The question of the origin of the Moon **is interesting** not only in itself but also as a part of the larger genesis of the Earth and the solar system.

Despite the evidence of the existence of small amounts of water vapor and ice crystals on Mars, its atmosphere **is known** to be extremely dry.

This phenomenon has been described so often as to need no further cliches on the subject here.

When birds are molting, normally once or twice a year, **they can be seen much less often.**

The constitution provides that **no president can be elected more than twice.**

59. **As soon as she saw me,** she turned red.

No sooner had she seen me than she turned red.

Hardly(Scarcely) had she seen me before(when) she turned red.

No sooner had I gone home than it began to rain heavily.

I had scarcely locked the door when the key broke.

Immediately(The moment, The Instant, The minute) she saw me, she became angry.

60. He **did not arrive until** it grew dark.

It was not until it grew dark that he arrived.

Not until it grew dark did he arrive.

61. There are **doctors and doctors.**

    There are **teachers and teachers.**

62. Important **as** sugar is, we can't live upon it.

    Woman as she is, she is so brave.

63. He came **from behind the bush.**

    The dog came **from under the bed.**

    The game didn't start again **till after dark.**

64. In his time he enjoyed a reputation **as great as Mozart, if not greater.**

    In his time he enjoyed a reputation **as great as, if not greater than, Mozart.**

65. If I **had** the opportunity, I **would like** to tell them why.

    I **would explain** it to her if I **thought** she would understand.

    But for water, no living thing **could exist.**

    If he **had answered** the detective honestly, he **would have been arrested.**

    Had he listened to me, John **would not have failed.**

    If the parents **had gone** to the meeting, they **could have discussed** the problems with the principal himself.

    With promptness, you might have arrived in time for the first act.

    It would have been wiser **to leave it unsaid.**

    If you **had studied** the problem carefully yesterday, you **wouldn't find** any difficulty now.

    If he **were** a good student, he **would have studied** for the test.

    If you **had listened to** me, we **wouldn't be** in danger.

    If I **had learned** the phonic system of reading, I **would be** a better reader today.

    If the United States **had built** more homes for poor people in 1955, the housing problems now in some parts of this country wouldn't be so serious.

    I wish professor Jones **had taught** me this equation.

    I sometimes **wish** that Deer Creek **were** not such a little town.

I **would have helped** her **but** I **didn't have** the money.

He **would gain** weight **but** he **doesn't eat** much.

She **would have gone except** she **didn't have** time.

The rose would have grown well **but** I did not water it.

Jean would go to New York **but** she has no money.

I would go to visit that beautiful lake **but I can't get in touch with you** while I am now in Boston.

66. Experts from the WHO have decided that **the time** has come **to study herbal medicine very carefully.**

All blades perish **that pierce the dreadful king.**

The time will come **when we will win the game.**

Many problems have developed **with their regulations.**

Several generalizations are made **from which several conclusions are drawn.**

67. **Returning to my apartment, I found my watch missing.**

Running along the street, I felt my nose frozen.

It being Sunday, I went to church.

This done, we went home.

To relieve the pain, the man took medicine that was prescribed by the doctor.

68. I regret **not working harder** while young.

I regret **not having worked** harder while young.

69. Why do you **object to following** the direction?

Mr. Brown often wore a heavy coat because he **was not used to living** in such a cold climate.

I **am looking forward to seeing** him next summer.

Vets have had to **resort to killing** the animals.

He **contributed to winning** the game.

70. John Bennet is president of an insurance company **and** his brother Frank is the state treasurer.

Jean had not realized **how long the magazine was or how difficult it was to read.**

The king was loved by his friends, respected by his subjects, and feared by his enemies.

In Scandinavian countries household goods are devised **both to function well and to look well.**

The tourists decided **not to make a trip to Virginia but to remain where they were.**

John never realized that in order to play the piano, he must have **not only training but talent also.**

I have enjoyed the study of the Spanish language **not only because of its beauty but also because of its use in business.**

71. He is difficult to please.(= It is difficult to please him.)

He is impossible to deal with.(=It is impossible to deal with him.)

* John is easy to master English.

72. I am always loving you.

She is being careful.

73. He quickly turned the pages.(= The pages were quickly turned by him)

He quickly turned the corner.(= *The corner was quickly turned by him)

74. the man who threw the bomb

(≠) the man throwing the bomb

the woman who looks after small children

(≠) the woman looking after small children

people who wish to succeed

= people wishing to succeed

people who get up early in the morning

= people getting up early in the morning

75. Pears are eaten **fresh, dried or canned.**

He came back home **safe and sound.**

He returned home **a gentleman.**

76. Next year's budget is **too** tight **to** renovate our branch office and to add the cafeteria proposed over a year ago.

He is **too** poor **to buy** the car.

According to our itinerary while visiting Seoul, our sales representative have **enough to meet** with as many as ten branch managers.

He has **enough** money **to buy** the car.

His explanation was **so** complicated **that** I could not understand it.

Airfares during the peak seasons are usually so high that I decided to work during the summer vacation period and take a week off in September.

77. We placed the order three weeks ago, but the company **has yet to give** us any detailed information on the delivery.

He **has yet to** finish the report.

78. Our goal is to improve **our employees' ability to compete with employees of rival firms.**

The manager has **the right to fire anyone in his division without explanation.**

He made **an attempt to stand up.**

Failure to obey the regulation may result in disqualification.

She was annoyed by **his unwillingness to do his share** of the work.

Their offer(plan, promise) to rebuild the town was not taken seriously.

79. Many, but not all, insects can see colors, though generally **a different array than humans perceive.**

He is **otherwise than** I **thought.**

Receptors for smell are used **differently than receptors for taste.**

I want to raise my children **differently than my parents did.**

80. Because he seldom wrote you doesn't necessarily mean he loves you no longer.

Since the richest part of a gold-bearing quartz vein is on the bottom, just because gold is not seen doesn't mean it isn't lurking just below eyesight.

81. **Change your mind as you will,** you will gain no additional support.

= Even though you change your mind, you will gain no additional support.

Hurry as you will, you are sure to be late.

= However you may hurry, you are sure to be late.

Call it a blessing or a curse of Mother Nature, we have to breathe in over 10,000 liters of air a day to remain alive.

Be a man rich or poor, he eats three meals a day.

Be it ever so humble, there is no place like home.

82. She was the first woman [to be elected / who was elected / elected] chair of the meeting.

He was the first man [who reached / to reach] California.

83. When fossil evidence of the soft anatomy is preserved, **it is not the original material that remains,** but rather only a stony replica of the former structure.

84. The police rounded the men (who were) **known** to have been in the building at that time.

The man (who is) **standing** over there is my friend.

The men (who were) **responsible** for the administration of the school refused to consider the matter.

He spoke to the man (who was) from New York.

85. I **happened to be looking** out of the window when they arrived.

He **seems to be following** us.

He **appears(seems) to be living** in the area.

He **pretended to be looking for** a book.

I **hope to be earning** my living in a year's time.

I **promised to be waiting at** the door when he came out.

He **is believed to be living** in Mexcio.

You **are supposed to be working.**(= You should be working)

You **are supposed to have been working.** (= You should have been working.)

86. Snakes, **unlike lizards,** do not have eardrums and are deaf to air borne sounds.

Freezing is at present **one of the most important methods** of preserving meats and vegetable.

The electron microscope **provides** researchers **a means of viewing objects** as small as bacteria or viruses.

The Pacific Ocean, **the world's largest body of water,** occupies about one-third of the Earth's surface.

Volcanoes spew forth **not only** molten rock **but also** huge amounts of carbon dioxide.

Willa Cather **considered** her novel of life in nineteenth -century Nebraska, My Antonia, **her best work.**

The last half of the nineteenth century witnessed the steady improvement of the means of travel.

One of the areas of multimedia **that is growing quickly yet is easily overlooked is sound.**

One difference between mathematics and language is that mathematics is precise **while** language is not.

They found the plan difficult to carry out.

We had plenty of bread, so I **need not have bought** a loaf.

So nervous did he get when he entered the room that he could hardly talk.

Who do you like to see be the Opening Day starter?

The building measures **20by 10by 10feet.(가로20 세로10 높이 10feet)**

She doesn't like **it** when new girls join her friends and try to change the way they jump rope.

I will go **only if** you go too.

If only (If) I had known his address, I would have written to him.

If only I were rich.

87. **Although(Though) he had no qualifications** he got the job.

= **In spite of having no qualifications** he got the job.

Because she was ill, she couldn't attend the party.

Because of her illness, she couldn't attend the party.

88. He is always **the first to come**(who comes) and **the last to leave** (who leaves).

She was **the only one to survive**(who survived) the crash.

He is **the last man to tell** a lie.

He is **the second man to be killed** (who was killed) in this way.

It is **the best play to be performed** (that was performed) that year.

It is **the best play to perform** (the play you should perform) this year.

89. (A) His greatest mistake **was** that he gave up his studies.

He **is** kind.

He **is** a doctor.

The choice **remains** difficult.

Without making a real effort you **will remain** what you have always been.

Our refusal **appeared** a serious mistake.

Our new line in sportswear **has proved** a great success.

The milk **turned** sour.

I **felt** bad this morning.

It **is getting** late.

The lemon **tasted** sour.

The meat **has gone** bad.

His dream **came** true.

He **won't be(make,*become)** a good doctor.

He **kept** silent.

In the fridge the milk will **keep** fresh for three days.

(B) Please **start** the clock going.

They **left** me waiting outside.

We must not **keep** them switching.

They **found** the man dying in the woods.

We **will find** Jerry waiting for us at the gate.

A few words **caught** in passing set me thinking.

The policeman **caught** a man stealing a car.

I can easily **remember(imagine, recall, picture)** Billy stealing a cookie from the jar.

(C) He **married** her.

He **survived** the war.

Please **contact** me.

It **threatens** the whole mankind.

They **attacked** me.

Please reconfirm your return flight schedule as soon as you and your staff members **reach** the next destination.

Over 60 species of fish are known to **inhabit** the waters around the Antarctic continent.

Papaya juice **relieve** several stomach disorders.

(D) Can you **explain** that to me?

She **introduced** her mother to me.

He **has already suggested** that to me.

She **is explaining** a problem to the student.

(E) He **gave** me a book.

He **mailed** her a letter.

She **informed** them **that she would come here.**

I **promised** my friend **that I would meet after two hours.**

* I **promised** my friend to meet after two hours.

He **told** me his name.

We **told** them **that we would be late.**

He **advised** me **whether I should choose the way.**

They **notified** the students **that they should meet at the hall.**

She **convinced** me **that he was honest.**

He **reminded** me **that the road was dangerous.**

He **showed** me **that it was quite easy.**

He **taught** me **that I should obey all commands without asking questions.**

(F) Tom **allowed** Mary to follow him.

You **are allowed** to smoke in the room.

They **forbade** you to learn Russian.

She **told** me to do my homework.

Last night, in a radio address, the president **urged** us to subscribe to the Red Cross.

She **asked** me to open the door.

Passengers flying on Korean Airlines **are asked to board** at Gate 24 at least 20 minutes prior to scheduled departed times.

* He hoped her to succeed.

He **hoped for** her success.

He hoped she would succeed.

I **got** him to repair my watch.

I **got** my watch repaired.

He **helped** her **to(ø)** do her homework.

We **encourage** our employees to study foreign languages.

The government announced deregulation and tax-deductible plans to **encourage** foreign businesses to invest more funds in the area.

(G) I **prevented** her from dating with the man.

Her illness **kept** her from going outside.

I **dissuaded** him from studying hard.

(H) He **insisted** that she should change her clothes.

He **insisted** that she changed her clothes.

He **demanded** that that bill should be passed.

Her expression **suggested** that she was angry.

(I) They **saw** him run across the street.

They **saw** him running across the street.

My mother **made** me visit my relatives before I came to college.

The police let the thief go.

He **was seen to run(running)** across the street.

I **heard** my name called.

I must **have** it fixed.

You ought to **have** your coat cleaned and pressed.

Please **get** the lawn mowed.

I **saw** our country's flag raised.

We had so many things happen to us.

I wanted to **make** my room look clean.

I **had(*made)** my hair cut.

I **had(*made)** my maid clean my room.

He **made** her do(*doing) her homework.

I **had** her drive(driving) all day.

(J) Frank **disclosed(revealed)** Cyril as having murdered Agatha.

* Frank **disclosed(revealed)** Agatha as having been murdered.

I **regard** John as being angry too often.

I **regard** John as being culprit.

* I **regard** John as speaking too often.

I **regard** John as being beaten by his wife.

(K) We **recognize** him to be reliable.

I **understand** that explanation **to be right.(*to be wrong).**

I **suspect** that man to be a liar.

* I **suspect** that man to be an honest man.

I **find** this chair to be uncomfortable.

I **find** this chair uncomfortable.

I **believe** him to be honest.

I **believe** him honest.

I **believe** him to be an honest man.

* I **believe** him an honest man.

I **believe** him to be a suitable candidate.

* I **believe** him to be a French teacher.

I cannot **imagine(*suppose)** how disappointed he was.

I **consider** him **to be a suitable candidate.**

I consider him **as a suitable candidate.**

I consider him **a suitable candidate.**

I consider **that he is a suitable candidate.**

(L) I just **love it** that you are moving in with us.

Rumor **has it** that he is honest.

I **hate it** that you like to lie.

We **agree to it** that she should join us.

You'll **see to it** that he will be punished.

(M) My shoes **want(need) mending.**

My shoes **need to be mended.**

The battery **needs(wants) replacing** once every three months.

= **needs to be replaced**

(N) * I **think** that she is not honest.

I **don't think** that she is honest.

It **is not likely** that she will come here.

* It is likely that she will not come here.

He doesn't **seem** to be rich.

(O) I **want** my shoes mended(to be mended).

I **prefer** coffee mixed(*to be mixed).

I'd **like** it boiled(*to be boiled).

(P) I **will walk** her home.

I **will walk** home.

She **talked** to him about starting a business.

She **talked** him into starting a business.

She **fasted** her illness off.

She **shouted** her head off.

She **slept** her fatigue off.

Many people **have eaten or drunk** themselves to death.

(Q) He **came** back home safe.

We **parted** the best friends.

He **returned** home wounded.

(R) I **think** that he is honest, isn't he?

You **think** that he will pass the test, don't you?

* I **know** that she is honest, don't I?(isn't she?)

Part (D) : Grammar Practice

* Correct the underlined part which is ungrammatical.

1. A good exercise program helps teach people to avoid the habits that might shorten the lives.

   Seminole Indian warriors wore egret feathers in hair.

   Zoologists have determined that each deer usually has many mates in the lifetime.

   Ella Grasso was the first woman governor in the United States to be elected on her own merit, not as a replacement for the husband.

   You are required to fasten seat belt loosely while seated, even when the seat belt light is off.

2. Classicism as a doctrine seeks what is universally truth and good.

   The leaves of the yucca are usually point, stiff, and narrow, with sawlike or fibrous edges.

   After 1845, pestilence spread in Boston, but before then, Boston was a city in which the life span of its citizens was long and disease was rarely.

   The jaws of female sawback turtles are broad, flat, and powerfully for crushing the shells of mollusks, one of their principal foods.

   The young of most bird species are totally dependence on parental care after hatching.

   In pools, goldfish are not just ornamental: since they feed on mosquito larvae, they are also benefit.

   When metals become heat enough, the photons their electrons emit contain enough energy to be visible to the human eye as red light.

   During the Jurassic period plant life was abundance, providing herbivores in particular with a plentiful supply of food.

   The arthropods, including insects and spiders, are great economic and medical significance.

3. Researchers at the University of Colorado are investigating a series of indicators that could help themselves to predict earthquakes.

   The vanilla vine sends out tiny rootlets by which the vine attaches oneself to trees.

   We expect everybody else to feel towards us that tender love and that profound respect which we feel towards ourselves.

   Plants rid them of excess water through transpiration, the evaporation of extra moisture from their leaves.

   Samantha received a bonus for the way she successfully handled the huge transaction by oneself.

   At the regular Friday meeting, the executives voted unanimously to give yourself another pay raise sometime during the next fiscal year.

   They placed their papers in front of them.(*themselves)

   He looked about him(*himself).

   She took her dog with her(*herself).

   I have no money with me(*myself).

4. A fish must constantly to gulp water in order to keep a current flowing through its delicate gills.

   A lightening flash produces electromagnetic waves that may travels along the Earth's magnetic field for long distance.

   The natural gas that flows from a well must to be cleaned and treated before being marketed.

   My understanding could not catching up with his explanation.

5. Muscular motion is caused by the stimulate of specific nerve cells in the brain and spinal cord.

   The waters of Hanauma Bay in Oahu, Hawaii, are known for the color, diversity, and abundant of their tropical fish.

   Entomologists, scientists who study insects, are often concerned with the fungus, poisonous, or virus carried by a particular insect.

   Settled in 1872 as a railroad station, the city of Fresco, California, became an agricultural community after the introduce of irrigation in the 1880's.

Recognition of the nutritional valuable of rice grain has led to increasing consumption of brown rice.

In 1917 Ruth Wheeler was appointed chairperson of a national committee on nutritiously for the American Red Cross.

Professor Marshall discussed the question with Professor Robert and I.

6. The first libraries in the North American colonies was established in Massachusetts in the year 1638.

Book keepers maintains detailed records of business transactions.

Some small magazines are put out by two or three persons, but the big, general publication are tremendously complicated operation.

The meticulously crafted works of Henry James, which often treat the theme of innocence and corruption, is characterized by subtle observation and psychological perceptiveness.

Navigation, the process both of determining a vehicle's position and of directing its movement, involve many sciences, including astronomy, mathematics, and physic.

The nectar of flowers are ingested by worker bees and converted to honey in special sacs in their digestive system.

Facts about the population of the United States is collected at ten-year intervals by a government census bureau.

Few of us realizes what a vast amount of information has been gathered about our feathered friends, the birds.

The news of the losses suffered by our troops were much worse than expected.

Already, cosmetics company in most cities have started to post higher sales figures than ever before, despite the recent prolonged recession.

A number of companies that need information about our product has e-mailed requests to our promotions division to get product brochures.

The number of nurses employed by Mount Sinai General Hospital on a quarterly basis are increasing due to the rising demand for medical care in the area.

7. Pewter, a metal with an ancient heritage, is still practical medium for the nonprofessional metalworker.

A principle of manager is to ensure that every action or decision achieves a carefully planned goal.

Alice Hamilton was physician who did pioneering work in industrial toxicology, the study of poisonous substances in the workplace.

Invented in 1907, the vacuum tube was basis to the development of long-distance radio and television communication.

Marine biology, the study of oceanic plant and animals their ecological relationships, has furthered the efficient development of fisheries.

The Architectural History Foundation was established in 1977 to support the publication of important book on architecture.

Most bats roost in crevices, caves, or building by day and are active at night or twilight.

Metalworkers use the term "machine tool" to refer to a piece of an equipment used for shaping metal.

Pears are eaten fresh, dried, or canned, and the wood of pear tree is used in cabinetmaking.

For a seagoing, cargo-carrying sailing vessels, the clipper ship was remarkably fast.

He wants to get an information about the accident.

The progress must be carefully controlled so that the company will not grow too fast.

Vaccines can provide protections from infection for an extended amount of time.

You can purchase tickets at consolidated ticket office at least two hours prior to the main performance.

Long before Dr. Young opened his own private clinic, he had studied to become physician for almost seven years.

8. According to cognitive theories of emotion, anger occurs when individuals believe that they have been harmed and that the harm was either avoidable and undeserved.

Social welfare programs in the United States depend not only on the federal government or also on the state government for resources and administration.

9. How Native Americans developed corn is a puzzling, for no wild corn has ever been discovered, and it grows only where people plant and tend it.

At the close of the Civil War, Peter Clark was the forerunner of a moved in Cincinnati to create new schools and to improve old one.

10. At end of the Civil War the United States was ready to resume with a roaring surge the westward expansion which had been interrupted for four years.

The eight stripes of red, white, and blue on state flag of Hawaii represent Hawaii' eight major slands.

Approximately 55 percent of the area of state of Mississippi is covered with forests.

Astronomy is a science of stars and planets.

He gave me a(the) book which he bought yesterday.

Eminent physicists from all over the world came to the United States to celebrate a centennial of Einstein's birth.

He turned on a television.

Gatherings of more than three persons were prohibited supposedly in the name of the law and order.

After the church the men stood together in the churchyard saying he must be crazy.

The resistance of insulators is so great for practical purposes they do not conduct electricity at all.

11. Most talc is used ceramics and roofing because it resists fire good.

Because he could not think clearer, his efforts in trying to solve the problem have failed.

To improvise effectively, a musician must thorough understand the conventions of a given musical style.

Some people say that a mushroom is edible if it can be peeled easy.

Although aging improves some foods, fish must be handled prompt and careful from the moment of the catch until final processing.

She still has not found her selection, though she has analyzed his desires perfect.

His trip was large political in nature, but, because he was an excellent businessman, his perception of what the world might be in the postwar years was strongly tinged with business insights.

12. The way of reasoning whereby people do conclusions by logical inferences from given premises is called the deductive method.

    The strong wind does a terrible noise when it blows through the antenna.

13. Helen Vendler's essays present key insights into and vital analyses the works of major British and American authors.

    Mr. John Smith has been appointed the new British ambassador of the U.N.

14. Documentary evidence indicates that portraiture became an established art form in the Hudson Valley region around the 1660.

15. Both the United States silver dollar and half-dollar, first minted in 1794, had a figure of Liberty on one side and a eagle on the reverse side.

    The International Monetary Fund was created in a effort to stabilize exchange rates without interfering with the healthy growth of trade.

    I held an opinion that a honest man who married and brought up a large family did more service than he who continued single and only talked of the population.

    Parsley, an(a) herb that is often added to sauces and soups, is plentiful and relatively inexpensive.

16. Little Rock, Arkansas, is the city with the most oldest newspaper in the United States west of the Mississippi River, the Arkansas Gazette, founded in 1819.

    The magnetic compass, which points to Earth's north magnetic pole rather than to true north, is the most commonest type of compass.

17. John Fitzgerald Kennedy, the first United States President born in the twentieth century, was also the first to win an election with votes east in 50 state.

In the late nineteenth century, journalist and publisher William Randolph Hearst established a vast publishing empire that included eighteen newspapers in twelve city.

Thousands of meteorite hit Earth each year, but most fall into the sea or in remote areas and are never recovered.

Rodents dwell in various habitat, some species being aquatic, some terrestrial.

Young chimpanzees can learn over 200 signs of American Sign Language and use this signs to communicate with humans.

The frequency of meteors in the Earth's atmosphere increases when the Earth passes through a swarm of particle generated by the breakup of a comet.

The Department of Fine Arts and Architecture has been criticized for not having much required courses scheduled for this semester.

All employee are required to wear their identification cards while on company premises.

According to a recent news article, there seems to be a lack of skilled engineers in many of the computer technology industry.

Medical experts have vowed to take every measures possible to eliminate the side effects of he new drug.

18. Because American contra dances date from the colonial period, many of them are named for events historical of that time.

The chemical properties of the elements various are quite diverse, their atoms combine in many different ways to form a multitude of chemical compounds.

A landmark famous, the Brooklyn Bridge in New York was one of the first woven wire cable suspension bridges ever constructed.

The human average takes 600 million breaths in a 70-year lifetime.

Cadmium is a useful chemical in the manufacture of artists' pigments, automobileenamels, vinyl plastics, in addition to phosphors for color television tubes.

It is dangerous to catch such fierce alive animals.

19. In music, syncopation is the deliberate upsetting of rhythm by shift the accent to a beat that is normally unaccented.

In sculpture, the term "modeling" refers to the technique of shape a soft material such as clay or wax.

Pasteurization is the process of heat a liquid, particularly milk, to destroy harmful bacteria without materially changing its compositions, or, flavor, or nutritive value.

Because the diamond is the hardest naturally occurring substance, it is used in industry for to cut, grinding, and boring other hard materials.

Solar salt is produced by use the Sun's heat to evaporate water that comes from the ocean or from inland salt lakes.

A calorie is the amount of hot needed to raise the temperature of one gram of water by one degree Celsius.

Martin Luther King, Jr. is well-known for organize the huge human rights march that took place in Washington in 1963.

After labor for weeks to reach an agreement, the two sides finally managed to come to a mutually beneficial conclusion.

Acquired education is the principal way of gaining status in a culture that generally stresses achievement, skillfulness, and upward mobility.

We regret to announce that the recent increase in sales taxes will result in a reducing in employee benefits.

By reduction our overhead expenses, we can offer more compensation to our employees.

She kept him from escape.

The embarrassed professor pleaded not guilty to the charge of drive while intoxicated.

20. Processed lecithin is used as an emulsifier in manufacturing margarine, chocolate, and another foods in which fats or oils must be mixed with water.

Saccharides, molecules composed of carbon, hydrogen, and oxygen, are the building blocks of sugars, starches, cellulose, and another carbohydrates.

I like another ink.

In order to make people change their feelings about this writer he has to write another books regarding this problem.

21. Many of United States presidents have served as state governors on their way to national leadership.

Many the students at Maryland University agreed that the campus's overall facilities were more than satisfactory but complained that more faculty members were needed to handle the increasing number of students.

Almost all of staff members are willing to relocate to the suburban area due to the abundance of office and parking space and the quieter working conditions.

Some of substances contract when they condense, but water expands.

Most of people eat rice rather than potatoes.

22. The Grand Canyon is over 217 miles long, some 4 to 13 miles width, and up to 5,300 feet deep.

The cork oak tree has layer of cork several inches thickness that can be stripped every ten years.

23. In its use of brilliant unmodulated color, optical painting overlaps with some, though not by no means all, aspects of color-field painting.

24. Twenty-five years after its founding in 1740, the University of Pennsylvania opened the first medically school in the thirteen British colonies.

Changes within the chemist structure of single genes may be induced by exposure to radiation and extreme temperatures.

Free land, cheaply transportation, and powerfully persuasive railroad advertising all helped floods the western part of the United States with farmers in the nineteenth century.

The musical tone of an electric guitar is created not by the resonance of the body of the guitar but by electronically amplification.

The dandelion plant has a straight, smoothly, and hollow stem that contains a white, milky juice.

The only way to reach the edge of the forest was to take the narrowly dirt path before us.

The carpenters built the speaker's platform strongly enough to hold ten men.

The doctor's records must be kept thoroughly and neatly, so as to insure good bookkeeping.

The door was painted whitely.

25. The development of computers has been one of the most important recent advance in technology.

Amnesty International, an international organization for the defense of human rights, is one of the few institution to have won a Novel Peace Prize.

26. By the gravitational effects of its mass, the Sun holds together the planetary system that include the Earth.

Most insurance companies adopt a commission system that pay sales representatives according to their performance.

Before we start the revision process, department heads should first identify applicable provisions in the handbook that needs modification.

We are not supposed to be responsible for any malfunction or breakdown that result from improper use of the equipment.

Man is an inquisitive and gregarious animal who wish to know what is happening in the world.

27. Petroleum is generally regarded as an altered form of organic matter who was incorporated in sedimentary rocks at the time of deposition.

Memberships in a family is determined by a combination of biological and cultural factors who may vary from culture to culture.

Gail Sheey's Passages, what discusses the continuing psychological development of normal adults, is a most profound and important book.

In the attempt to control inflation by eliminating social programs, there are ethical limits beyond where many economists and politicians are reluctant to go.

The architect's task is to design buildings what are functional and beautiful.

Neither the God he served nor the learning he preserved counted for much in the world from whom he had retired.

Although I expected something different, I was still surprised by which he said.

The senior executive which began working for Natural Cosmetics twenty-seven years ago will retire by the end of this month.

This map does not show the exact location of the company who offers the most reasonable rates for one-day delivery service.

28. More a third of all the vegetable matter in the world contains cellulose.

For more eighty years, scientists have argued over whether life exists on the planet Mars.

29. According to modern astronomers, the space between the planets and stars is not empty; rather he is filled with something called dark matter.

Beyond their importance as a source of food for both people and animals, corn is also used to produce alcohol-based fuels.

Protecting Florida's coral reefs is difficult because some of the corals are very fragile: even the touch of a diver's hand can kill it.

It is difficult to classify mathematics as simply an art or a science because they contain elements of both.

People are usually interested in seeing a famous movie personality just as they are in real life.

It was during the 1920's that the friendship between Hemingway and Fitzgerald reached their highest point.

In spite of their aloofness and independent bearing, the domesticated cat has come to depend upon man for food and protection.

The weeks of summer training are often as tense for sports writers as it is for football players and coaches.

The good statesman, like all sensible human beings, always learns more from their opponents than from supporters.

In order to obtain a driver's license in this state, one has to present your birth certificate as proof of age.

Garlic is an herb grown for his pungently flavored bulb, which is used to season foods.

Our urge to classify different life forms and give us names seems to be as old as the human race.

Business managers should not only emphasize profits but think about what it can do for impoverished people with the money they make.

The problems that sales representatives have when they visit customers are similar to the one customer service staff have experienced.

30. Some of the first aerial photographs were taken from a balloon while the Civil War in the United States.

While his lifetime, Frederick Jones was awarded more than sixty patents for his invention.

31. Ludmilla Tukevich, known as a translator and scholar in the field of Russian literature, she became a member of the faculty of Princeton University during the Second World War.

The Canadian province of Alberta it is believed to have some of the richest oil deposits in the world.

32. Brown rice has great nutritional value than white rice because the nutrient-rich outer layers of the rice kernel are not removed from brown rice.

The Montery Foreign Language Center claims that its language training program is much more effective as that of other educational institutions.

33. Cool temperature, shades, moist, and the presence of dead organic material provide the ideal living conditions for mushrooms.

When the Moon enters the Earth' shadow, clouds, dust, and pollute affect its color and brightness, usually making it appear a dull red.

34. In music, a sequence is defined as a musical phrase immediate repeated at a different pitch.

Gold is exceptional malleable, and it can be hammered into a very thin sheet.

Since the early 1900's, the New York Public Liberty has been wide recognized as a pioneer in the field of children's educational and recreational activities.

35. Consequently sharks are heavier than water, they must swim continuously or they will sink to the bottom.

However I informed the travel agent of my revised schedule, the tickets he sent to me still show the previous dates.

Even the huge shopping mall appeared some six months ago, most of the stores have still not been leased out due to the high rents.

36. By 1830 the glass industry in the United States had become too well established that the country no longer needed to depend on imported glass.

Rubber can be made too elastic that it will stretch more than nine times its normal length.

37. The sensation of sound is produced how vibrations transmitted through the air strike the eardrum.

38. Much desert plants are succulents, plants with fleshy tissues used for water storage.

Of the much factors that contributed to the growth of international tourism in the 1950's, one of the most important was the advent of jet travel in 1958.

So much people attended the vice CEO's retirement party that some people had no place to sit.

Ever since the new software was installed, we have experienced few trouble responding to clients' requests.

39. One of the earliest plants domesticated in the Western Hemisphere, manioc was introducing to Europe by Spaniards returning from the New World.

The main stream of a river frequently is dividing into two or more branches near its mouth.

40. Recently scientists have apply new tools of biochemistry and molecular biology to investigate the structure of human hair.

Research in molecular biology has demonstrate phenomenal similarities between humans and apes.

41. The tall three beautiful Chinese girls came to visit us today.

Women also played a large part in our great first private relief organization.

42. Would you like any hot coffee?

No one on the committee had flatly made some such allegation, though Wayne

He is taller than some other student in his class.

He's never interested in what somebody else has to say.

The mediator was asked to resign after any union members raised questions about his competence and neutrality.

43. There has been hardly no sign of agreement as yet between the management and the union in their dispute over wages and working conditions.

The contractor agreed to build the apartment complex without removing a single tree or changing the terrain in no way.

I didn't see hardly many people there in the museum.

44. In the early of common man during the nineteen century, the objective was not merely to secure political privilege but also economic advantages for the underdog.

45. You should go to the third gate.

Please write out the answers to the questions at the end of eighth chapter.

46. He has only a two-weeks vacation during the year despite the fact that other workers get more time off.

Some bloods types are quite common, others are regionally distributed, and others are rare everywhere.

Where are the women hats?

The winner photograph was of an old barn window covered with a delicate, lacy frost.

I have finished a day work.

In the early intelligent tests, it was possible for a person to get a good mark if he knew enough root words, suffixes, prefixes.

Reversals may be caused by brain's injury.

47. Two weeks are too long for me to wait.

Five years has passed since he died.

48. The committee adhere to its decision to limit the evidence.

The family never agrees about their share of the property.

49. Those of us who wear glasses should have their eyes examined at regular intervals.

Those of us who wish to stay in shape should get their blood pressure checked regularly.

50. All during his political career, Senator Baker believed that it was the nation's welfare that mattered, not him.

Is the climate of Italy somewhat like Florida?

Scientists have recently argued that Einstein's contribution to physics and mathematics is as important as Newton.

51. Numerous efforts have been made to improve the laws governing air pollution, but none have been as successful as them devised by the state of Oregon.

William the Conqueror built the Tower of London to protect himself from them he had conquered.

For them interested in nature, the club offers hikes and overnight camping each week during the summer.

No one is allowed on the premises except employees and them who have a valid identification card.

Many flowers have smells that attract the birds or the insects that help fertilize those.

For them expecting to see Dr. Kim without an appointment, refer to the consultation schedule posted on the wall.

52. The question whether it is so or not might be interesting, but there is next to no evidence neither any.

He seldom, if any, studies English.

Rarely if any did a joke last more than 24 seconds.

53. The most of the theories about its origin assume that the earth began in a gaseous state, moved through a liquid state, and finally became partly solid.

Bernhard understands the most of the calculus equations, but he wants to study them again before the test.

William Sardo reported that the most oil refineries were in the black last quarter.

54. Like a synonym of speech, which is the general term, address implies some degree of formality.

As every other nation, the United States used to define its unit of currency, the dollar, in terms of the gold standard.

Alike other academic discipline, sociology has several major subdiciplines.

55. It wasn't enough good to fit it.

I think David will arrive enough early.

56. Mr. Smith did not get up until eight-thirty that morning and he arrived at the meeting late too much.

When preparing goods for shipment, do not put much too merchandise in one box; instead, pack four or five items each in separate boxes.

Some staff members think that the revised procedures are too much difficult for our newcomers to follow.

57. We play often that game, too.

There will be always problems here.

Music is extremely nearly always important.

He doesn't still understand Spanish.

58. As soon as I saw the smoke, I called the fire department, but they haven't arrived already.

No inventor has already built a musical instrument to match the ingenious flexibility of the human vocal tract, with its rubbery, marvelously mobile walls.

We missed the first part of the seminar because, when we arrived at the center, it had still begun.

Although he started working for this company some five years ago, he already has problems handling some of the most basic ordering procedures.

59. He is going to home.

A detailed map of the mining camp was handed out, and the directions for getting to there were repeated very clearly.

60. I think he is kinder than wise.

She is shyer than unfriendly.

61. 61. If you had taken my advice before doing the work, you would have been able to do it more better.

There are a number of areas in north central Pennsylvania that are more wilder than any other Eastern area outside the Smokie.

62. The intelligence ability of an athlete is usually far more than they would expect.

Aside from the resolution to have more ecumenical conferences, the most accomplishment of the group was that it met at all.

The population of Korea is less than that of America.

The attendance of the audience was more than we expected.

63. We should find a solution before things will get worse.

I shall go to Las Vegas before you will come back next week.

I will tell her when I will see her.

Let's go to the country tomorrow if it won't rain.

If you do follow my advice, I don't punish you.

We can do nothing unless she will consent next week.

Our purchasing department will check the invoice and forward the payment as soon as we will receive our order dated March 1.

When you will complete this workshop, you must take a simple test to see if everything presented here has been fully understood.

I don't know if she comes here tomorrow.

64. They would come out to attack and then disappeared back into the deep forests, where their opponents were at a disadvantage.

After searching for evidence in the house, the police concluded that the thief must have come in through the window and stole the silver while the family was asleep.

He was standing quietly when presently a young woman, who had been combing her hair and watched him, approached and asked him for directions.

When he was a little boy, Mark Twain would walk along the piers, watch the river boats, swimming and fish in the Mississippi, much like his famous character.

He hoped they would learn from their mistake and obeyed the rules in the future.

My father enjoys fresh air, sunshine, and to take long walks.

65. Coffee is my favorite hot drink, even though it <u>kept</u> me awake at night.

Almost every morning I receive cards inviting me to art exhibitions, and on the cards <u>had been</u> photographs of the works exhibited.

Weighed down by a mass of trivial detail, a housewife is fortunate if she <u>did not soon lose</u> all her charm and three-quarters of her intelligence.

She <u>visited</u> twice since March 1969.

Since we adopted Theory Z management practices, productivity <u>rose</u> by nearly 20% and absenteeism <u>fell</u> by more than 50%.

In the last decades movie production <u>advanced</u> with great strides.

Although I have lived in this country <u>after</u> last September, I still have trouble getting used to American food.

When I went back to my office after a month-long sick leave, I found that one of my best associates <u>fired</u> a week earlier.

I wonder how long ago this school <u>has begun</u>.

I think she <u>studies</u> English right now.

In just the last few years, football <u>is become</u> more popular than baseball in that country.

The instructor had gone over the problems many times before the students <u>take</u> the final examination.

By then I <u>will finish</u> my work.

When he retires, Professor Jones <u>will be teaching</u> here for over thirty years, but his classes are never dull.

Mr. Lee <u>have served</u> as senior accountant for almost 20 years by the time he retires.

Oberlin College <u>awards</u> degrees to both sexes as early as 1837, but coeducation in American colleges did not spread until the second half of the century.

In the past ten years, the number of college graduates with degrees in mechanical engineering and computer science <u>had risen</u> by almost 20%.

66. I suggest that he follows my advice.

Jean's uncle insists that he doesn't stay in this hotel.

He requested that we must not watch television on week nights.

The committee recommended that the matter would be discussed at the next meeting.

When he was asked why his friend had not accepted the offer, he suggested that his friend's pride should prevent him from accepting.

It is natural that an employee finishes his work on time.

It is imperative that they shall be there on time.

I think it advisable that he will leave for Tokyo soon.

It is strange that you will say such a thing.

For environmental reasons, it is important that dead batteries are disposed of properly.

67. He also told of frightened events that had taken place in his native state of Connecticut.

Not too many years ago, it was an excited experience to travel 25 or 50 miles from home.

Understanding the cultural habits of another nation is a complex bewildered task, but the rewards of knowing some of them are enormous.

On Sunday, after visiting other interested parts of the city, Mary will go to the airport and fly home.

At last we found the exhausting animal lying there, sick.

68. It was such a beautiful weather that we had gone for a walk.

We heard so long lecture that we were falling asleep.

As time went on, he suffered so heavy losses that he was forced to give up his business.

The theme park has had so high daily attendance throughout the year that we are considering developing more facilities for school outings next year.

69. It is more better.

There are much more examples here.

Using the two drugs in combination produces many stronger results than when either is used alone.

They require many more money.

70. She did nothing but to complain.

There is nothing to do but to wait.

I can't do otherwise than to obey him.

I have no ambition except be rich.

We have no other choice but surrender.

Nothing remains but die.

All you have to do is to pay me what you owe me.

What you should do is to stick it out.

I can do everything around the house except to cook.

I had no choice but do as he told me.

71. It was good something.

It was an impossible mission.

He was a man honest.

It is an alive animal.

72. Can you finish your homework until tomorrow?

I shall wait by ten o'clock.

73. Handicapped people frequently state that they feel isolated and other people avoid them.

According to cognitive theories of emotion, anger occurs when individuals believe that they have been harmed and the harm was both avoidable and undeserved.

74. This is the most beautiful city that I have never visited so far.

It is a long time since you didn't come to see me.

75. Gauze is a thin, open-weave clothes made of cotton, silk, rayon, or synthetic fibers.

76. Doctors tell us that stress related illnesses from stomach ulcers to heart attacks are the biggest cause of death and disability in 1990's.

77. Some members of the committee were opposed to use the club members' money to redecorate the meeting hall.

Pearl S. Buck International(PSB) is a non-sectarian development and humanitarian assistance organization which is dedicated to improve the quality of life for children.

After dealing with the pressure of publication deadlines for many months, Catherine has now become used to allocate her time efficiently to multiple tasks.

78. There are a great many stars in the sky which are too far away from the earth of any instrument to detect.

It is difficult of him to solve the problem.

It is kind for him to say so.

79. Even though the two subsidiaries have few commercial ties, that is certain that they will cooperate with each other quite closely.

The screening process conducted by the personal division will make easier for board members to review resumes for qualified candidates and to make quicker hiring decisions.

We found simpler to follow the installation procedures in this new manual and have therefore decided to translate it into four languages and distribute it to our respective overseas dealers.

80. Almost accountants have already submitted their CPA credentials, and the rest are supposed to turn them in no later than September 24.

The park is surrounded by tall trees, almost of which were planted during the city's modernization project in the late 1980's.

81. For smart buyers wanting to make better decisions on their purchases, that is seen in commercials is not necessarily important in their decision-making process.

What it took only two months to complete construction of the airport is certainly an amazing record, and the construction crew deserve recognition for what they have accomplished.

82. Because the firm's long-standing reputation, enjoyed for nearly a decade, the newly launched camcorders are selling quite well, even without any advertising.

Because of complicated issues were involved, the project was delayed.

Because the damage caused by the tornado, production was suspended for almost a whole month.

Despite we are still experiencing a shortage of employees in our accounting division, the reduced budget keeps us from hiring anyone for the time being.

We still want to purchase imported home-theater units rather than buy those manufactured locally, even though the high costs involved.

Overseas sales of electrical appliances soared more than 30 percent during Jim McBride was working as sales manager.

No one under the age of eight is permitted to view the exhibition without accompanied by a paying adult.

If you use our convenient on-line service rather than phoning us, you can enjoy unlimited access to all our information around the clock, unless having to wait for a representative to answer the phone.

83. All passengers traveling overseas must be arrived at the airport at least one and a half hours prior to their scheduled departure times.

As a long-term investor, what has been happened in the stock market over the past month and a half has not really influenced my decision-making.

84. Sally is a woman <u>you can depend</u>.

The children <u>were not taken care</u> by their parents.

Who do you want me <u>to talk</u>?

85. Body temperature is usually highest <u>inside</u> the afternoon or evening.

The period during <u>when</u> people learned to smelt iron is called the Iron Age.

Sharing corporate stocks with employees can be an effective way to promote <u>harmonious</u>, efficiency, and equitability in the workplace.

Tons of boulders were <u>leaved</u> scattered by glaciers all over what was to become the New England landscape.

Perception is the complex process by which we <u>selection</u>, organize, and interpret sensory stimuli into a meaningful view of the world.

<u>Most</u> serious than burlesque, satire often contains social or political criticism.

High interest rates can dampen an economy by making it more <u>difficulty</u> for consumers, businesses, and home buyers to secure loans.

Skin is <u>largest</u> but thinnest human organ.

Why the piratebush is so rare, even though there is many habitats suitable for its survival throughout the Appalachian Mountains, continues to puzzle scientists.

Air is expelled from the lungs when the chest muscles and diaphragm relax and the lungs <u>contraction</u>, squeezing out the air.

When light shines on a material, interaction with atoms and molecules in the material may cause the light to be absorbed, <u>reflect</u>, transmitted, or scattered.

Although many tornadoes are sighted each spring in the Midwest, few of <u>they</u> ever touch the ground or do much damage.

The discovery of x-rays in 1895 allowed doctors <u>get</u> a clear picture of a patient's bones without surgery.

Absolute color <u>blind</u>, which is rare, causes a person to see only black, white and various shades of gray.

Among Amy Hempel's <u>distinguish</u> features as a writer are her humor and keen ear for speech habits.

The tempting, or toughening, of steel involves reheating the metal to a temperature below the point to which was first heated.

An electromagnet will remain magnetized only as longer as electricity flows through it.

The first ocean to be extensively navigated by humans the Indian Ocean.

Amelia Bloomer founded, edited, and publication The Lily, the first newspaper devoted to women's rights.

The bigger of all nine planets in the solar system is Jupiter.

Generally, the summers in Pennsylvania have very hot and the winters are extremely cold.

The idea that learning is a lifelong process has been expressed by philosophers and educations throughout the centuries.

The benefit of goat's milk lies in the fact that it is more easily to digest by infants and invalids than is cow's milk.

Physician and the poet William Carlos Williams often expressed resentments at having to practice medicine to pay the way for his writing.

Because the Oregon Trail passed through long stretches of barren country, people and animals alike frequently faced fatigue and hungry.

Machines vary in complexity, ranging from so simple devices as the crowbar and wheelbarrow to the more complicated elevator, automobile, and printing press.

Many nineteenth-century opera arias bring together a memorable melodically, a dramatic interlude, and a leading character in a moment of high artistry.

Beside the ages of nine and fifteen, almost all young people undergo a rapid series of physiological changes.

Emily Dickinson, among the greatest women poets in the English language, died with all of hers poems unpublished, except for seven that appeared in publications of limited circulation.

The guide has recommended that we both are as attentive as possible when we visit the old castle.

Plants of these type grow best in places where there is a great deal of shade.

The uneducated is more to be pitied than blamed.

Do you think its going to rain tomorrow?

Would you mind me trying that coat on for size?

You will have to make the curves rounder : otherwise, everyone will be copying your mistakes.

She said that her son went slowly to school everyday.

Inevitable and maybe unfair comparisons are likely to be made between the sales manager in Oakland and his counterpart in Fargo.

The following night Bill returned quite lately from work to find his wife lying unconscious beside the phone.

The prime minister's conviction for improper campaign practices is likely to result in increasing pressure that she resigns.

To become a member of the civic association, one need only attend three meetings and to pay his fees regularly.

That nitrogen is indispensable to plant and animal life.

Neither John and his father was able to wake up early enough to catch the morning train.

The reason I didn't go to France was because I got a new job.

Ohio has long been a leader into the invention, improvement, and manufacture of farm machinery.

During nearly fifty years superconductivity defied explanation and was one of the outstanding puzzles of physics.

Except special exhibitions, most museums in the United States have no admission charge.

New automobiles are designed to run on low-octane fuel containing little or none lead.

Playing jokes on April Fool's Day is a common practice in many regions, although none knows how the tradition began.

Modern advertising is as frequently used to promote ideas and positions as it is to sale products.

Mother's Day is on May.

Part (E) : Actual Test

* Identify the correct one.

1. I spent the day taking (photographic, photographs, photographer) of the city.
   They produced a (photographic, photograph, photographer) record of the event.
   She is one of the most famous fashion (photographic, photograph, photographers) in the world.

2. The article is full of (inaccurate, inaccuracy, inaccurately).
   All the maps we had were wildly (inaccurate, inaccuracy, inaccurately).
   A Gallup poll released yesterday is said to be taken (inaccurate, inaccuracy, inaccurately).

3. The term I used was meant to be purely (describe, description, descriptive).
   The man was (described, description, describing) as tall and dark, aged about 20.
   The police have issued a (describe, description, descriptive) of the gunman.

4. Money is not (essence, essential, essentially) to happiness.
   The pattern is (essence, essential, essentially) the same in all cases.
   Her paintings capture the (essence, essential, essentially) of France.

5. His (include, inclusion, inclusive) in the team is in doubt.
   The tour (includes, inclusion, inclusive) a visit to the Science Museum.
   The rent is (include, inclusion, inclusive) of water and heating.

6. They considered the (relate, relative, relationship) merits of the two plans.
   I found it difficult to (relate, relative, relationship) the two ideas in my mind.
   The (relate, relative, relationship) between the police and the local community has improved.

7. The student took many (use, useful) courses in college.

   The (use, useful) of cameras is forbidden inside the museum.

   John (uses, useful) a vacuum cleaner to clean the carpet.

8. Anne submitted the form with the (require, required, requirement) signature.

   This job (requires, requiring, requirement) a college degree.

   The candidate met all of the (require, required, requirement) for the job.

9. Susie is (responsibility, responsible, response, respond) for feeding the family dog.

   Taking care of a younger sister is too much (responsibility, responsible, response, respond) for a six-year-old child.

   The judge asked the witness to (responsibility, responsible, response, respond) to the question.

   As a (responsibility, responsible, response, respond) to my question, Mary said she was angry at me.

10. Successful candidates should have a (minimum, minimize, minimally, minimal) of five year's experience in accounting.

11. All employment (applications, applicability, applicant) must be postmarked before Oct.31.

12. According to the chemist's (interpretations, interpret, interpreter), the constitution used in this kind of detergent is very harmful.

13. Most of the toys are on a big post-holiday (sell, sale, selling, sold).

14. It is not easy to find any (differ, different, differently, differences) between the two materials.

15. The (producing, product, productive, production) schedule was changed due to the delay in the shipment of materials.

16. The fire chief said their estimated time of (arriving, arrive, arrives, arrival) was in four minutes.

17. A number of job (openings, gap, aperture) were posted in the newspaper.

18. However, thanks to careful (planned, plan, planner, planning), the downtown area is coming alive again.

19. The Rocky Mountain region is an area of (interesting, interests, interested, interest) in the United States.

20. People with these kinds of certificates have more (possibility, probability, chances) of being hired.

21. When ordering any entree, you have your (choice, option, decision) of vegetables.

22. The research company started to look into media (coverage, covering, cover, coveraged).

23. We'd better find a market with (fewer, least, a few, less) competition for these products.

24. We are notifying you that your September payment is 36 days (outdated, advanced, overdue).

25. A (living, alive, lively, live) broadcast was televised from New York last night.

26. You should consider investing in an (expand, expanse, expansion, expansive) view.

27. I am sure this goal will be reached in the (foreseeable, foreseen, foresight, foreseeing) future.

28. Of the two candidates, Mr. Spiers is (more, the better, the best).

29. Due to the economic downturn and poor business, the executives of the company recommended (early, previous, past) retirement to the employees.

30. The (opposing, opposed, opposes) view should always be considered and sometimes taken.

31. The response was (satisfactory, satisfied, satisfying) and most of the attendance consented to the speaker's point of view.

32. My new boss was so (understanding, understandable, understood) that he was willing to approve my sudden vacations.

33. He is such a pleasant co-worker that getting along with him is (eager, willing, happy, easy) to do.

34. The new system is quite (impressed, impressive, impression).

35. (Them, Those, Themselves, Whichever) who need advice on their career options can visit the Job Center anytime between 9 and 5 on weekdays.

36. A lot of accidents can be (prevented, restrained, constrained) by turning on your headlights before it gets dark.

37. We were (explained, informed, spoken) that our flight would be delayed due to minor mechanical problems.

38. The vice president insists that we (is, had, be, been, are) redesigned.

39. When he (suggested, told, recommended) me about the accident which happened to Mr. Lee, I was shocked.

40. These sports wears (stated, designed, aimed) at young adults.

41. You should consider all aspects when you decide (exact, exactly, exacting) what to buy.

42. (Neared, Nears, Nearly, Nearing) ninety percent of the hotel rooms were reserved for weekends this season.

43. Some companies are (continually, lastingly, timelessly) dumping pollutants in the sea without any environmental consideration.

44. His car had been (hard, hardly) used when he decided to sell it because he lived near a subway station.

45. I have not (already, still, yet) met the new staff transferred from the New York office las week.

46. (It, There, They) remain four possible solutions.

47. We have to spend the allocated amount as (efficient, efficiently, more efficient) as possible.

48. You should be as (attentive, attention, attended) as possible during class.

49. The luggage he packed up for his trip is (much too, too much) heavy.

50. They should speak (clear, clearness, clearly).

51. They are charging (them, they, theirs, their) clients.

52. (Almost, The most, Most) of them are members of the standing committee.

53. He doesn't have (a, the, any, some) qualms about the workers though he laid off nearly twenty of them.

54. I could help (hers, her, herself, hers) finish the project this Saturday morning.

55. One task is already taken care of, but there is (any other, either, another) waiting for us to be done.

56. She was shocked when she saw (her, herself) in the mirror.

57. The company will place an order for office supplies (as, such as, such, along with) a ruler, an eraser.

58. (Even although, Although, Despite, Nevertheless) they were not prepared enough, they launched the new program.

59. The applicants (who, whoever, which) had an interview with the vice president yesterday got the position.

60. (As well as, In addition, Moreover) carrying excessive amounts of alcohol and cigarettes, having fresh fruit can be illegal.

61. (Aside from, Except that) golfing every weekend, he enjoys a lot of sports.

62. The sales representatives are going to demonstrate the new products (in, on, at) April 23.

63. We will move to the new head office in the center of town (until, by, on, during) the end of next week.

64. They will meet (at, in, on, to) the corner of Seventh Street.

65. (Since, In spite of, Due to) there was low attendance, the president had to cancel the next seminar.

66. The undergraduates, many of (them, whom, that, which) will go on to teach math at high school, all did well during their internship.

67. He studied so hard to pass the bar exam (before, while, for, after) the last three years.

68. You can contact our office to have your name placed (by, on, at, to) the waiting list.

69. You'll miss the bus (in case, unless, given) you walk more quickly.

70. Demand for new van is (such, very, so, such a) high that further orders can't be filled till next Jan.

71. We had (such, so, such a, too) high attendance we were excited.

72. (However, How, Whatever) hard you may try to find the breakthrough for this recession, the current trend for downsizing will continue for the time being.

73. You can meet the people (who, whoever, whom, whose) family members suffered from it for a long time and get some helpful advice from them.

74. The shop remains open (by, on, until) 9 o'clock.

75. You can leave the office (as long as, as far as, so far as) you can finish the work.

76. It still remains (being, been, have been, to be) seen whether Michael Gartenberg will get a contract because the competition is stiff.

77. Plants need (to be watered, to water, being watered) 5 times after planting and then they can generally make it through the summer.

78. New York police reported that the 29-year-old man (was fired, has been fired, fired, had been fired) from a factory shortly before the incident.

79. The reduction in salaries (has, have, are, is) angered all employees.

80. Mr. Smith (will serve, will have served, serves, served) the full two years in office as president by the time his last term ends.

81. If the board of directors refuses to combine Balloons and its subsidiary, the company (goes, will go, went) bankrupt.

82. The employees (will send, will be sent, send) to our branch office.

83. The company (has introduced, was introduced, introducing) a new water- proof watch.

84. Students are expected (to registering, to register, registering) at the front desk.

85. They must sign out and (initial, initiative, initials) their attendance records.

86. 86. I had barely (finishing, finished, finish) the work.

87. Had Mr. Toth (elected, been elected, electing) as a chairman, the company would have gone into bankrupt.

88. The construction project was (processed, processing, completing, completed) as planned.

89. Helium and hydrogen are (light, lighter, lightly, lightest) than oxygen.

90. (The, No, If) wrong use of this medicine may lead to accidents.

91. Some information (gave, was given, given, giving) in this package will be specified in a few handouts.

92. This project is the (most challenging, more challenging, challenging) program in our company.

93. You can take short trip to Las Vegas before (return, returned, returning) home for $50 only.

94. He finds Picasso's paintings (fascinating, fascinated, to fascinate).

95. Interns should not be afraid of becoming (disappointed, disappointing, disappointment).

96. She encourages employees (participating, to participate, participation) in the annual meeting.

97. Once (merge, to merge, merged, are merged), the companies will create more profits.

98. Anyone (ordered, orders, who order, ordering) art supplies must initially undergo customs inspections.

99. (No sooner, No soon, As soon as) had Mr. Cho left the institute than the door closed.

100. In order to (saving, save, saves) time, he does not spare any efforts.

101. (Impaired, Injured, Wounded, Damaged) luggage should be brought to our office.

102. The company is considering (to introduce, introducing, introduce, introduced) a new line.

103. (An, The) equipment is required to be serviced every month.

104. (Developed, Developing, Development, Develope) effective training is necessary.

105. (Many of, Many of the, Many a) customers who know us are repeat customers because of our good quality and reasonable price.

106. The consultant whom Ms. Carson (talked to, talked, talked of) was helpful in changing her occupation.

* Choose the one that best completes the sentence.

1. ______ should be given to those whose applications are received by next Tuesday.

   (A) Preferential (B) Preferred (C) Preference (D) Preferring

2. As soon as the contract for the ________ of Central Hospital is signed, the two old buildings will be demolished.

   (A) constructing (B) construct (C) constructive (D) construction

3. With fresh water sources dwindling, the proper _________ of water distribution systems is now more critical than ever before.

   (A) utilization (B) utilizable (C) utilize (D) utility

4. Companies should ensure that employees' ________ is measured not by test results alone but also by efforts demonstrated on the job.

   (A) performance (B) performing (C) performed (D) perform

5. We regret to announce that the recent increase in sales taxes will result in a ________ in employee benefits.

   (A) reduction (B) reducing (C) reduced (D) reducer

6. By ______ our overhead expenses, we can offer more compensation to our employees.

   (A) reduction (B) reducing (C) reduced (D) reducer

7. The government's decision to increase defense _________ by some 20% indicates that tension does exist between North and South Korea.

   (A) spending (B) spend (C) spent (D) spender

8. Our Find-it-for-You service posts numerous job ________ from entry to management level.

   (A) open (B) opens (C) opened (D) openings

9. Everybody in the division considers Martha to be the most successful and ________ accountant.

(A) reliability (B) reliably (C) reliable (D) reliance

10. Although the antibiotics helped the patient at first, in the end, the virus proved to be completely ________.

(A) resistant (B) resistance (C) resisting (D) resisted

11. Yearly sales for the new cosmetic line have significantly increased, although the demand for specific products varies ________ at different times of the year.

(A) considering (B) considered (C) consideration (D) considerably

12. In today's meeting, everyone is ________ encouraged to offer at least one suggestion on how we can best compete with rival companies like Hewlett Packard.

(A) strong (B) stronger (C) strongly (D) strongest

13. The photocopier that we purchased just before Christmas has proven to be as ________ as the Xerox sales representatives had promised.

(A) reliably (B) reliable (C) relied (D) relying

14. With the help of our newly designed electronic invoicing system, your accountant ill be able to process customer transactions as ________ as any large business.

(A) efficiencies (B) efficient (C) efficiency (D) efficiently

15. Employees who fail to submit the required information on their families within two weeks ________ their dental care benefits.

(A) forfeiture (B) will forfeit (C) forfeiting (D) forfeits

16. My associates and I would like to extend ________ congratulations on your recent promotion and invite you to visit our new office soon.

(A) my (B) our (C) your (D) their

17. With __________ proven track record and competence, everyone agrees that Mr. Chang deserves the promotion to office head.

(A) he (B) his (C) him (D) himself

18. The accounts we offer this month boast more customized individual services than ________ offered last month.

(A) that (B) those (C) this (D) these

19. As a start-up venture company, we have only three branches nationwide and a total of 25 employees, most of ________ are graphic designers.

(A) them (B) whom (C) who (D) that

20. Although it is statistically ____________ to fly than to drive, many people are nevertheless afraid of flying.

(A) safer (B) more safely (C) safe (D) safest

21. The industry-mandated quality tests were much stricter than ________ .

(A) expectation (B) expected (C) expect (D) expecting

22. Of the two resumes that we reviewed yesterday, Mr. Vickson's seems to be the __________.

(A) best (B) better (C) good (D) well

23. _________ had Carrie arrived in Rome than her purse was stolen.

(A) Sooner (B) The sooner (C) Any sooner (D) No sooner

24. We will neither cut the number of full-time workers ___________ reduce their overall benefits.

(A) but (B) or (C) and (D) nor

25. It is mandatory to _________ a work identification card when you first enter the company.

    (A) obtain　(B) obtaining　(C) obtains　(D) obtained

26. The value of the dollar ____________ yesterday against the Japanese yen after skirmishes in the Middle East died down.

    (A) rising　(B) to rise　(C) risen　(D) rose

27. The proposed budget increases would make it possible __________ added support to each sector of them.

    (A) give　(B) gave　(C) to give　(D) in giving

28. Although I'm _________ about your situation, I have to consider the best interests of this company.

    (A) empathetic　(B) empathize　(C) empathizing　(D) empathically

29. ________ the new supervisor is mild-mannered and soft-spoken, she is very firm about getting work done on time.

    (A) Even　(B) Then　(C) However　(D) While

30. To achieve success in today's competitive environment, companies must a solid business plan.

    (A) to establish　(B) establishing　(C) establish　(D) establishes

31. Real estate values have been __________ from year to year in most parts of the United States.

    (A) rise　(B) rose　(C) risen　(D) rising

32. The Chief of Security ____________ to us that we should take the highest precautions to ensure no information was leaked to the press.

    (A) informed　(B) convinced　(C) notified　(D) mentioned

33. The council __________ the director that continued support of the Baker project might result in financial loss.

(A) advised (B) explained (C) recommended (D) announced

34. The Trattoria Restaurant requests that patrons __________ reservations for a table at least two weeks ahead of time.

(A) makes (B) making (C) made (D) make

35. Due to the urgency of this matter, it is imperative that Mr. Lambert one of our customer representatives by 5 p.m.

(A) is contacting (B) will contact (C) contact (D) contacted

36. The recent meeting between the two companies _________ that a deal is near.

(A) imply (B) implies (C) was implied (D) implied

37. The federal government, along with the cooperation of leading industrial companies, ________ to create more jobs for skilled workers.

(A) is pushing (B) are pushing (C) pushing (D) have been pushed

38. The number of users who __________ support has increased since the company released the latest version of its software.

(A) require (B) requires (C) is required (D) are required

39. This year the car industry __________ many investors because automotive products now make up 15 percent of the country's exports.

(A) attract (B) has attracted (C) attracting (D) had attracted

40. The e-mail addresses and telephone numbers should be _________ carefully in the blanks provided.

(A) written (B) write (C) wrote (D) writing

41. The accounting team is __________ to providing accurate billing statements and resolving all customer inquiries within twenty-four hours.

(A) dedicating (B) dedicated (C) dedicate (D) dedication

42. If the client had come on time, these negotiations ________ completed by now.

(A) would be (B) would have been (C) won't have been (D) would not be

43. Had the contract __________ earlier, we might have been able to discuss the conditions and make a decision before the week's end.

(A) deliver (B) delivered (C) been delivered (D) were delivered

44. The firm temporarily closed one of its branch offices ______ operating expenses.

(A) will reduce (B) reduces (C) reduced (D) to reduce

45. ________ regular donations to local charities from business profits is not only personally rewarding, but good for developing a reputation.

(A) Give (B) Gives (C) Giving (D) Given

46. The chef obtains interesting and different results with this dish by ________ the ingredients he uses in the recipe.

(A) vary (B) varying (C) varied (D) varies

47. It would be wise of you to consider ________ with your firm, as the job market is tough right now.

(A) signing (B) sign (C) to sign (D) signed

48. Customers who hear music on an open telephone line ________ on hold are less likely to hang up.

(A) to (B) as (C) nearby (D) while

49. A number of our staff were late coming to the office today ________ the East bound A-train got stuck on the tracks.

(A) if (B) because (C) that (D) unless

50. Electronic communications make it possible to do business ________ you are in the world, whether in or out of the country.

(A) whenever (B) whomever (C) wherever (D) whatever

51. Our office can begin filling out the order ________ the completed request form and Instructions are sent via fax.

(A) once (B) just (C) upon (D) still

52. ________ the company has been selling the same product for thirty years, it is still popular with consumers all over the country.

(A) In light of (B) Nevertheless (C) Therefore (D) Even though

53. Management has decided to rotate workers to keep the assembly line running as ________ as possible.

(A) efficiency (B) efficiently (C) more efficient (D) efficient

54. Unfortunately the shipment will be delayed, as our factory is experiencing more technical problems ________ we anticipated.

(A) or (B) while (C) whether (D) than

55. Of the many laborers at this plant, the ________ highly skilled will be transferred to a newly opened facility.

(A) so (B) most (C) such (D) much

56. The responsibilities of a representative include __________ the company's sales goals and managing the special requests of customers.

(A) to achieve (B) achieving (C) achieved (D) achievement

57. Had we ___________ that the event would not be a popular one with our customers, we would have dropped the plan in its early stages.

(A) realize (B) realized (C) been realized (D) realizes

58. _________ the firm's poor performance, its CEO, Paola Guashin continued to expand its facility.

(A) However (B) Nonetheless (C) Despite (D) Even Although

59. The objective of this course is to help you function more effectively in your job and to be more _________ in the job market.

(A) competition (B) competence (C) competitive (D) competitor

60. I have not ____________ made any false statement or deliberately misleading omission in completing this license application form.

(A) knowingly (B) knows (C) known (D) knowledge

61. Every year since the governor __________ four years ago, he has delivered the Friday luncheon speech.

(A) had elected (B) is electing (C) was elected (D) will elect

62. One of the two candidates accepted our offer and will be joining the faculty this summer, while __________ candidate declined the offer because of dual career constraints.

(A) others (B) other (C) the other (D) the others

63. We usually use the expedited service available which guarantees __________ in seven days maximum.

(A) deliver (B) delivery (C) delivered (D) deliverable

64. For a creative advertising __________ to be successful, the ad will need to be simple and consistent throughout and target the key audience that you want to reach.

(A) strategic (B) strategy (C) strategize (D) strategical

65. Reservations which are not guaranteed by credit card at time of booking are subject to ________ by the hotel without prior notice.

(A) be canceling (B) cancel (C) cancellation (D) canceled

66. I have not yet found time to read the monthly production report ________ due to the preparation for the upcoming marketing strategy meeting for next year.

(A) me (B) mine (C) myself (D) my

67. All meetings should be scheduled at a time and place _________ to a majority of the Committee members.

(A) accept (B) acceptance (C) acceptably (D) acceptable

68. The custom-designed packaging was created ________ for this lifelike doll.

(A) exclusively (B) exclusive (C) excluding (D) exclusion

69. I'm writing to thank you for allowing me the opportunity to meet with you today ___________ the position of financial advisor with your company.

(A) regard (B) regards (C) regarding (D) regardless

70. Little effort has been _______ to solve the problem so far.

(A) called (B) asked (C) made (D) done

71. It is essential that new ideas in music, drama or scenic design ___________, otherwise it will become a stuffy, fossilized musty repository of out of date ideas.

(A) admitting (B) admit (C) admitted (D) be admitted

72. Our resources are very limited, ________ we have to make sure that the services we arrange for people are efficient and cost-effective.

(A) so (B) as (C) furthermore (D) although

73. The Institute currently has three medical officers, all of __________ are widely respected working specialists.

(A) what (B) which (C) them (D) whom

74. _______ often employers insist that their decisions about their workers have nothing to do with color, gender, age or other factors, many workers don't believe them.

(A) However (B) Whatever (C) Whenever (D) Wherever

75. A simultaneous interpretation system will be used on this site _________ visitors will not run into language barriers.

(A) in order (B) so that (C) despite (D) now that

76. In August of the current year in _________ with the similar period of the last year, industrial production grew by 12.8%.

(A) comparable (B) comparing (C) comparison (D) compared

77. You must turn in the projects on time, _______ extreme situations.

(A) including (B) except from (C) barring (D) bar

78. PowerPoint 97, the current version, lets you make your presentation more _______ .

(A) power (B) powerful (C) powered (D) powering

79. You have four business days from citation issue date to pay a parking ________.

(A) fine (B) rate (C) charge (D) fee

80. A growing number of companies have ________ adopted climate-related targets.

(A) voluntary (B) volunteer (C) voluntarily (D) volunteering

81. Aspirin use ________ in patients who have heart disease since last year.

(A) has increased (B) have increased

(C) is increased (D) had increased

82. You can do this as ________ as you'd like until you get the results you want.

(A) quick (B) frequent (C) common (D) often

83. The most ________ part in the President's speech was when he outlined his strategy for the next five years.

(A) interest (B) interested (C) interesting (D) interestingly

84. If you had ________ me that it was her birthday yesterday, I would have bought her some flowers.

(A) reminded (B) remembered (C) repeated (D) recalled

85. The government intends to reduce the amount of the ________ paid to people without jobs.

(A) benefits (B) rewards (C) advantages (D) wages

86. I am trying to ________ the number of applications I have sent in the last three weeks.

(A) work (B) work out (C) work up to (D) work away

87. Recent statistics show that __________ companies operating in this field reduce costs by outsourcing part of their activity.

(A) most (B) most of (C) the most (D) mostly

88. Three __________ employees went on strike and demonstrated to protest against the restructuring plan.

(A) thousands of (B) thousand of (C) thousands (D) thousand

89. Household consumption has been falling gradually for the last six months, _______ worries some financial analysts.

(A) which (B) what (C) who (D) that

90. It took me several months to get used to ________ my messages by email.

(A) send (B) sending (C) have sent (D) be sent

91. With the new software, our accountant will no longer need to spend so much time ________ new data.

(A) enter (B) to enter (C) entered (D) entering

92. There is too _______ time left to get the report ready before the meeting.

(A) little (B) few (C) many (D) some

93. It's high time we _______ where to hold the next annual conference.

(A) decide (B) decided (C) have decided (D) are deciding

94. I have been looking all over for my passport. I cannot find it ________.

(A) nowhere (B) anywhere (C) somewhere (D) everywhere

95. If they had designed a more advanced product at an attractive price, they _______ a larger market share.

(A) had gained (B) will have gained

(C) would have gained (D) would have been gained

96. The young intern who was hired last month is quite _______ about accounting.

(A) known (B) knowing (C) knowledge (D) knowledgeable

97. The advertising agency suggested ________ the spring sales campaign at the end of March.

(A) that we start (B) us to start (C) to start (D) start

98. Although we had left home on time, we arrived at the airport much than we expected.

(A) late (B) later (C) lately (D) latest

99. We have four elevators in this building but _________ seem to be working this morning.

(A) neither of them (B) none of them

(C) both of them (D) all of them

100. You cannot access ___________ where all the financial transactions are made unless you are a staff member.

(A) the room (B) in the room (C) to the room (D) into the room

101. As he was afraid of missing his flight, the manager ________ his assistant to drive him to the airport.

(A) made (B) had (C) got (D) let

102. Ms. Brown answers the phone and replies to my e-mails when I am on ______ abroad.

(A) appointment (B) assignment (C) average (D) travel

103. From now on we will have to work much ______ to improve the quality of our components.

(A) hard (B) harder (C) hardly (D) as hard

104. They will use ______ very sophisticated equipment for the presentation.

(A) a (B) many (C) few (D) some

105. The ______ from Paris to London takes less than two hours.

(A) fly (B) travel (C) journey (D) fare

106. It will take several years to repair ______ damage caused by the hurricane.

(A) a (B) few (C) many (D) the

107. They will sign the contract ______ you give them a better discount.

(A) provided that (B) in addition (C) instead (D) prior to

108. Most of our employees ______ today because of the strike.

(A) worked (B) is not working

(C) are not working (D) have not working

109. Mr. Cooper ______ a conference at the moment.

(A) attends (B) attended (C) is attending (D) have attended

110. He ________ to drive since he had an accident.

(A) has not been able (B) could not

(C) cannot (D) is not able

111. If it rains this weekend, we ________ to cancel the barbecue.

(A) had (B) might (C) will have (D) would have

112. I'm thinking ________ a small house by the sea.

(A) to buy (B) to buying (C) of buying (D) to have bought

113. It is essential that you ________ here on time tomorrow.

(A) be (B) was (C) to be (D) will be

114. I can't paint the ceiling myself. I will ________.

(A) have been painted (B) have it to paint

(C) have it painted (D) have it paint

115. That yellow hat really makes him ________ stupid.

(A) look (B) to look (C) looking (D) looked

116. Don't forget ________ me when you arrive at your hotel.

(A) phoning (B) phoning to (C) phone (D) to phone

117. The new card allows you ________ cash at any ATM around the world.

(A) withdraw (B) to withdraw (C) withdrawing (D)for withdrawing

118. The annual conference will ________ in Munich next year in June.

(A) hold (B) be held (C) be holding (D) have held

119. Let me introduce you to Ms. Smith who is the personal assistant _________ Mr. Johnson.

(A) of (B) to (C) at (D) from

120. She always talked about her new job so __________ that we never suspected she was going to resign.

(A) exciting (B) excited (C) excitedly (D) excitement

121. The new head office is _________ 25 miles away from the main airport.

(A) locating (B) locate (C) located (D) location

122. Our company is not _________ to face a hostile tender offer from its main competitor.

(A) enough large (B) large enough (C) as large (D) larger

123. Statistics show that most prices _________ by about 5% when the new currency was introduced.

(A) rise (B) raise (C) rose (D) raised

124. It was _________ a boring presentation that a lot of people left the room before the end.

(A) so (B) such (C) very (D) too

125. If demand for this product continues to increase at this rate, we will probably have to _______ new staff this summer.

(A) take on (B) take away (C) take in (D) take over

126. The prototype that __________ last week does not comply with international standards.

(A) presented (B) is presenting (C) was presented (D) was presenting

127. Battery-operated reading lamps _______ very well right now.

(A) sale (B) sold (C) are selling (D) were sold

128. Many employees seem more _______ now about how to use the new telephone system than they did before they attended the workshop.

(A) confusion (B) confuse (C) confused (D) confusing

129. The prime minister is expected to arrive at the convention hall at _______ 7:00 P.M.

(A) approximately (B) approximates (C) approximate (D) approximated

130. Dr. Abernathy's donation to Owston college broke the record for the largest gift _______ given to the campus.

(A) always (B) rarely (C) once (D) ever

131. The lecture will cover the relevant methods of _______ the impact of currency fluctuation on international transactions.

(A) determination (B) determined (C) determining (D) determine

132. Answering telephone calls is the _______ of an operator.

(A) responsive (B) responsibly (C) responsible (D) responsibility

133. The president of the corporation has _______ arrived in Copenhagen and will meet with the Minister of Trade on Monday morning.

(A) still (B) yet (C) already (D) soon

134. Employees are _______ that due to the new government regulations, there is to be no smoking in the factory.

(A) reminded (B) respected (C) remembered (D) reacted

135. It has been predicted that an ________ weak dollar will stimulate tourism in the United States.

(A) increased (B) increasingly (C) increases (D) increase

136. ________ has the marketing environment been more complex and subject to change.

(A) Totally (B) Negatively (C) Decidedly (D) Rarely

137. That is the position for ________ Mr. Kaslov has applied, but a final decision has not yet been made.

(A) which (B) whom (C) that (D) what

138. Executives of small companies earn ________ salaries on the west coast than on the east coast.

(A) more (B) taller (C) richer (D) higher

139. You need about forty different nutrients to stay ________.

(A) health (B) healthy (C) healthily (D) healthiness

140. It is worth examining the ________ nations can take to facilitate the removal of trade barriers.

(A) stages (B) levels (C) steps (D) grades

141. Most people become nervous when ________ to speak before a large group of people.

(A) ask (B) to ask (C) asking (D) asked

142. ________ documents have to be sent in duplicate.

(A) All of (B) All of the (C) Every (D) The whole

143. I've had ________ personal problems recently to be able to concentrate on work.

(A) too many (B) so many (C) too much (D) so much

144. The first year's sales of the new calculator were so ________ that the firm decided to withdraw it from the market.

(A) discouragement (B) discourage

(C) discouraging (D) discouraged

145. Ms. Lee did ________ good work on that project that she was quickly offered a promotion.

(A) too (B) such (C) so (D) much

146. ________ higher ticket prices this year, attendance at area theaters remains above average.

(A) Even though (B) Nevertheless (C) In spite of (D) Consequently

147. Private financing can ________ a variety of forms.

(A) do (B) take (C) make (D) occur

148. The satellite photographed a ________ moon in orbit around Saturn.

(A) previous undetecting (B) previously undetecting

(C) previous undetected (D) previously undetected

149. Dr. Marsha Herbert's illustrations were clear enough to make her presentation ________ understandable.

(A) easily (B) easier (C) easy (D) ease

150. ________ in the late 1800's, many of the coastline's lighthouses remain standing today, having withstood the forces of nature for decades.

(A) Built (B) Building (C) Been built (D) Having built

151. Dr. Johnson is offering a three-hour workshop during ________ she will share some perspectives on effective time management.

(A) whose (B) while (C) whatever (D) which

152. A lot of environmental activists have been ____________ of the government negligence.

(A) critic (B) critical (C) critically (D) criticize

153. Magnum Plus cameras __________ very popular right now because they are so easy to use.

(A) became (B) are becoming (C) to become (D) becomes

154. A new marketing strategy was adopted but _________ overall effectiveness will be recognized sometime next year.

(A) they (B) it (C) its (D) them

155. Mark Javela, a junior employee, proposed an innovative project that has been funded by one of the organization's biggest _________.

(A) sponsor (B) sponsors (C) sponsored (D) sponsoring

156. Mr. Hermandez is not available at the time the work crew is scheduled to arrive, and _______ is Ms. Hakkonen.

(A) so (B) nor (C) neither (D) either

157. The National University plays an important __________ in preparing leaders for the country' educational system.

(A) work (B) piece (C) role (D) task

158. Intercity Bus Company will be providing ___________ bus service for holiday travelers next weekend.

(A) frequent (B) often (C) numerous (D) really

159. ________ all the candidates applying for the job, Mr. Wang appears to be the most promising.

(A) On (B) Between (C) Through (D) Of

160. The analyst's commentary in the progress report was sharply __________ of the leadership team.

(A) critical (B) critic (C) critically (D) criticism

161. After Massey Corporation acquired Brawley, Ltd., the _________ of its stock rose twenty percent.

(A) valuable (B) valuate (C) valued (D) value

162. The announcement __________ all employees to wear protective eyewear when using the machine.

(A) cautioned (B) caution (C) cautious (D) cautiously

163. Most universities have an active student life program for international students to make them more _______ in a new culture.

(A) comfortableness (B) comfortable (C) comfort (D) comfortably

164. Car rental expenses _________ among different companies because some charge for the day, and others charge per mile.

(A) vary (B) variation (C) variable (D) various

165. Russian companies are scheduled to outline their __________ plans for the development of their networks.

(A) strategic (B) strategies (C) strategize (D) strategically

166. The larger side view mirror was removed because it __________ obscures the driver's ability to see pedestrians.

(A) part (B) partial (C) partially (D) partiality

167. The __________ created briefcase organized for employees of the Denmark Publishing company is a show of appreciation.

(A) exclusive (B) exclusion (C) excludes (D) exclusively

168. The director of marketing was very surprised that the promotions assistant had completed the project ________ quickly.

(A) too (B) such (C) so (D) much

169. The company's advertising division _________ over 2,000 new customers with a successful new advertising campaign.

(A) attracts (B) was attracted (C) attract (D) has attracted

170. There are a number of websites available that _________ academic success by encouraging better time management.

(A) promote (B) promoted (C) promotes (D) to promote

171. Please _________ out this patient medical history form before the doctor comes in to see you.

(A) filling (B) filled (C) fill (D) fills

172. The company suggested _________ competitors with unprecedented access to its technology.

(A) provide (B) to provide (C) providing (D) provided

173. The Sweet Dream Pillow has been developed specially for those who frequently have difficulty ________.

(A) sleeping (B) sleeps (C) slept (D) to sleep

174. My assistant, Ken, is known for his ability ________ lost files and documents on computers.

(A) locate (B) have located (C) will locate (D) to locate

175. ________ the local dialect is the key to avoiding this kind of unfortunate situation; you should practice with your co-workers.

(A) Understand (B) Understanding (C) Understood (D) To understand

176. The recent flood disaster makes it impossible ________ Resort Management to promote property expansion at this time.

(A) of (B) for (C) from (D) if

177. Ms. Farriano recommended that we ________ Mr. Sidney as a representative of the company for the sales conference.

(A) were selecting (B) select (C) were selected (D) would select

178. Kristen Gerhart, who ________ the company's branch office in Washington, had a lunch meeting with the CEO yesterday.

(A) run (B) runs (C) running (D) were running

179. When the storm arrived, most of the local residents ________ the area.

(A) evacuating (B) have evacuated

(C) had evacuated (D) been evacuated

180. Our productivity has gradually been increasing ________ newer, faster computers were installed at the beginning of this year.

(A) as (B) due to (C) owing to (D) because of

181. Booksellers produced substantially different results after __________ asked to prepare a sales forecast of the highly anticipated new book.

(A) being (B) was (C) were (D) been

182. If our company __________ various air purification systems, consumers will be able to get more choices.

(A) introduces (B) will introduce
(C) to introduce (D) had introduced

183. An important thing to remember when __________ is to be patient and not sell your stock at the first sign of trouble.

(A) investigation (B) investing (C) invest (D) invested

184. __________ wisely you resolve the current friction with the supplier, you will never be able to be on good terms as before.

(A) Which (B) Whichever (C) How (D) However

185. Because of stricter grading, twice __________ students failed their introductory courses this year as last year.

(A) as many (B) much more (C) more than (D) too much

186. The fast food industry is facing financial difficulties in the __________ competitive worldwide market.

(A) increasing (B) increasingly (C) increase (D) increases

187. Despite some earlier __________ about dates and times, we've got it settled now.

(A) confused (B) confusing (C) confusion (D) confuse

188. The firm is looking for a candidate __________ strengths include the ability to work under pressure and solve problems creatively.

(A) that (B) what (C) which (D) whose

189. Clothing __________ directly from a distributor cannot be returned for cash, only for credit.

(A) bought (B) buyer (C) buy (D) buying

190. The most serious social problem plaguing the metropolis is its ________ population.

(A) large (B) many (C) much (D) grand

191. Could you tell me where I might find a ________ restaurant?

(A) tasty (B) delicious (C) good (D) spicy

192. Many modern novels have ________ recognizable plot.

(A) no (B) not (C) none (D) never

193. Nancy envied the way her brother could make ________ more friends than she.

(A) many (B) much (C) rather (D) a bit

194. They add ___________ less contamination to a vacuum than the best diffusion pumps.

(A) much (B) even (C) no (D) many

195. The cost is ________ much for me.

(A) so much (B) very much (C) too much (D) much too

196. After the oil embargo, no longer ___________ gasguzzling cars as the cost of gasoline increased.

(A) people could afford (B) that people could afford

(C) could people afford (D) could afford

197. I would wear my red dress save it _______ a stain in the front.

(A) had (B) has (C) would have (D) has not

198. If you had seen the amount of food he ate for breakfast this morning, you _______ why he has grown so fat.

(A) would understand
(B) would have understood
(C) will understand
(D) have understood

199. He could not go out with her until ________.

(A) they allowed to do so
(B) she allowed to do so
(C) he allowed to do so
(D) allowed to do so

200. Our general approach to __________ with companies is to go out our way to appease upset customers.

(A) deal
(B) dealing
(C) be dealt
(D) have dealt

201. The restaurant chain uses refrigerated trucks to transport meat and fresh _______ to its processing plant.

(A) produce
(B) produces
(C) production
(D) producers

202. Store loyalty cards that offer card-holders discounts and rewards are an effective way to _________ customers satisfied.

(A) keep
(B) do
(C) stay
(D) have

Actual Test 정답

* Identify the correct one.

1. photographs, photographic, photographers
2. inaccuracy, inaccurate, inaccurately
3. descriptive, described, description
4. essential, essentially, essence
5. inclusion, includes, inclusive
6. relative, relate, relationship
7. useful, use, uses,
8. required, requires, requirement
9. responsible, responsibility, respond, response
10. minimum
11. applications
12. interpretations
13. sale
14. differences
15. production
16. arriving
17. openings
18. planning
19. interest
20. chances
21. choice
22. coverage
23. less
24. overdue
25. live
26. expansive
27. foreseeable
28. the better
29. early
30. opposing
31. satisfactory
32. understanding
33. easy
34. impressive
35. Those
36. prevented
37. informed
38. be
39. told
40. aimed
41. exactly
42. Nearly
43. continually
44. hardly
45. yet
46. There
47. efficiently
48. attentive
49. much too
50. clearly

51. their
52. Most
53. any
54. her
55. another
56. herself
57. such as
58. Although
59. who
60. As well as
61. Aside from
62. on
63. by
64. at
65. Since
66. whom
67. for
68. on
69. unless
70. so
71. such
72. However
73. whose
74. until
75. as long as
76. to be
77. to be watered
78. had been fired
79. has
80. will have served
81. will go
82. will be sent
83. has introduced
84. to register
85. initial
86. finished
87. been elected
88. completed
89. lighter
90. The
91. given
92. most challenging
93. returning
94. fascinating
95. disappointed
96. to participate
97. merged
98. ordering
99. No sooner
100. save
101. Damaged
102. introducing
103. The
104. Developing
105. Many of the
106. talked to

* Choose the one that best completes the sentence.

1. C
2. D
3. A
4. A
5. A
6. B
7. A
8. D
9. C
10. A
11. D
12. C
13. B
14. D
15. B
16. B
17. B
18. B
19. B
20. A
21. B
22. B
23. D
24. D
25. A
26. D
27. C
28. A
29. D
39. C

31. D
32. D
33. A
34. D
35. C
36. B
37. A
38. A
39. B
40. A
41. B
42. B
43. C
44. D
45. C
46. B
47. A
48. D
49. B
50. C
51. A
52. D
53. B
54. D
55. B
56. B
57. B
58. C
59. C
60. A

61. C
62. C
63. B
64. B
65. C
66. C
67. D
68. A
69. C
70. C
71. D
72. A
73. D
74. A
75. B
76. C
77. C
78. B
79. A
80. C
81. A
82. D
83. C
84. A
85. A
86. B
87. A
88. D
89. A
90. B

91. D
92. A
93. B
94. B
95. C
96. D
97. A
98. B
99. B
100. A
101. C
102. B
103. B
104. D
105. C
106. D
107. A
108. C
109. C
110. A
111. C
112. C
113. A
114. C
115. A
116. D
117. B
118. B
119. A
120. C

121. C
122. B
123. C
124. B
125. A
126. C
127. C
128. C
129. A
130. D
131. C
132. D
133. C
134. A
135. B
136. D
137. A
138. D
139. B
140. C
141. D
142. B
143. A
144. C
145. B
146. C
147. B
148. D
149. A
150. A
151. D
152. B
153. B
154. C
155. B
156. C
157. C
158. A
159. D
160. A
161. D
162. A
163. B
164. A
165. A
166. C
167. D
168. C
169. D
170. A
171. C
172. C
173. A
174. D
175. B
176. B
177. B
178. B
179. C
180. A
181. A
182. A
183. B
184. D
185. A
186. B
187. C
188. D
189. A
190. A
191. C
192. A
193. A
194. A
195. D
196. C
197. B
198. A
199. D
200. B
201. A
202. A

대학생을 위한
기초영문법의 이해

발 행 일 2024년 6월 1일 발행

저 자 김우형, 김태영

발 행 인 송기수
발 행 처 도서출판 GS인터비전
편 집 인 송진우
편 집 처 도서출판 GS인터비전
표지디자인 디자인봄
인 쇄 처 더블비
등록번호 제 25100-2016-000050 호
전 화 02-976-7898
팩 스 02-6468-7898
이 메 일 gsinter7@gmail.com
홈페이지 gsintervision.kr
주 소 서울 은평구 증산로 15길 69, 2층
I S B N 979-11-5576-478-7(03740)

정가 25,000원

도서출판 GS인터비전